52 Homestead Skills

1503 S.W. 42nd St.
Topeka, KS 66609, USA
Telephone (785) 274-4300
Fax (785) 274-4305
www.ogdenpubs.com

First Edition. Copyright © 2018 by Ogden Publishing
All rights reserved.

No part of this work may be reproduced or transmitted in any form or by any means, electrical or mechanical, including photocopying, or by any information storage or retrieval systems, without written permission of the copyright owners.

ISBN: 978-0-941678-99-5

Printed in the U.S.A

The Journey Begins

Fueled by dreams of living a self-reliant, personally fulfilling, and independent life, the modern homesteading movement is running in high gear. Wages have more or less stagnated (adjusted for inflation) since the 1970s, while folks have seen expenses climb, work-conditions deteriorate — and employers escalate further extraction by suggesting that "workers should feel lucky to have a job." When less compensation for more work becomes the mainstream, the "less is more" movement grows in both appeal and power. Taking that philosophical plunge and embracing homesteading in the 21st century doesn't necessarily mean checking out of society or modern civilization, but the movement is driven by pioneers like Kimberlee Bastien and her family who find themselves trading an extractive consuming lifestyle for something that's simpler and way more complicated at the same time.

Embracing the work of living is what 21st-century homesteading is all about. Doing rather than buying can readily give a family some level of independence from the world where cash is needed to purchase all of the goods and services and stuff that one needs to occupy the house they don't have time to live in because they are too busy working to pay for everything. Some folks never get beyond dreaming about homesteading, some folks create a precise transition plan, and others basically hold hands and jump off the cliff right into the thick of it — tackling issues as they arise. The end result creates a passionate community, filled with doers and supportive dreamers who come together to encourage, help, and celebrate with one another. Wow!

No matter how you do it, the transition from conventional consumption-based lifestyle to homestead dreamer to homesteader can be daunting — particularly when you get into the thick of it. Imagine taking all of your conventional resources and putting them into a piece of land you intend to survive on, largely through doing for yourself. If you simply take the plunge, you might find yourself freezing in the winter, sweltering in the summer, and possibly even starving! Even if you plan meticulously, you might find yourself in the same situation. But hold on. Isn't that precisely what our ancestors did when they came to North America? It's no secret they needed help from home, help from the indigenous communities, and a lot of hard work to make it. Sprinkle a little good luck on that mess and plenty of them actually thrived and continue to do so.

There are still lessons to be learned from those very same ancestors — they were specialists in local economies, sustainable households, food gathering/production, and ultimately community building. Twenty-first-century homesteading isn't about regressing back to the dark ages; it embraces a paradigm shift that looks back to when the home was a place of laughter, love, and productive work that nurtured the fundamental human spirit.

We sought out Kimberlee Bastien for this project because she embodies the modern homesteader's spirit in a most compelling way. Adopting more or less the "jump off the cliff" approach, she and her family have embraced the daily, monthly, seasonal work of actually living! Organized into chapters describing particular homesteading challenges that required the learning of skills to meet, the reader gets more than just a glimpse of what goes into the homesteading transition. Here at MOTHER EARTH NEWS, Kimberlee is a pioneer hero!

— Oscar H. "Hank" Will III
Editorial Director, MOTHER EARTH NEWS
Co-owner/Operator, Prairie Turnip Farm

Contents

January • Page 6

- 10   Cooling Peppermint Deodorant
- 12   30-Minute Mozzarella Cheese
- 16   Seeds, Secrets, and Eating Only What You Grow
- 20   Spinning Yarn

February • Page 24

- 28   Cowstall to Chicken Coop
- 32   Homemade Laundry Soap
- 36   All Natural Dish Soap
- 38   Starting Seeds Indoors: Bonus Skill

March • Page 42

- 46   Build a Beehive
- 50   How to Light a Smoker
- 54   'Success'ion Planting
- 56   Controlling Garden Pests with Crop Rotation

April • Page 60

- 64   Raising Ducks for Eggs
- 68   Building a Duck House
- 72   Going Back to Eden
- 74   Beginner Bar Soap

May • Page 78

- 82   Gluten Free Sourdough Bread
- 86   How Not to Plant a Raspberry Cane
- 88   How Not to Grow a Fruit Tree
- 92   Compost

June • Page 96

- 100   Inspecting Your Hive
- 104   Foraging for Wild Edibles
- 108   Cooking from Scratch and in Season

July • Page 114

- 118   Raising Chicks

- 122   Building a Chicken Chunnel
- 124   Chickens for Fertilizer, Mowers, and Pest Control
- 128   Chocolate Mint Strawberry Freezer Jam
- 130   How to Use a Scythe

August • Page 132

- 136   The Great Bee Escape
- 138   Finding the Queen Bee
- 140   Honeycomb into Beeswax
- 142   Honey Hand Salve
- 144   Homemade Lip Balm
- 146   Remove Honey Filled Frames and Harvest Honey

September • Page 150

- 154   The Art of Fermentation
- 158   Water Bath Canning
- 162   Feeding Your Bees
- 164   Drying Herbs

October • Page 168

- 172   How to Milk a Goat
- 174   Dried Sweet Apple Rings
- 176   Homemade Yogurt
- 178   Starting a Grow Op
- 182   Saving Your Seeds

November • Page 186

- 190   Learn to Knit
- 192   How to Prune a Fruit Tree
- 196   How to Grow Lemons Indoors
- 202   Sweet Lemon Honey & Thyme Cough Syrup

December • Page 204

- 208   How to Make Butter
- 210   Homemade Candles
- 214   Homesteading with Little Humans
- 218   Getting Out of Debt

JANUARY

Crackling fires, hand knit socks, wool blankets, steaming cups of apple cider ... this is how I pictured homesteading in our Canadian winter. Sounds like a dream, doesn't it? It was.

As I looked out the window there were several feet of snow on the ground and the temperature read -32°C. The temperature in our 200-year-old farmhouse also read -32°C. OK, I'm exaggerating, but I'm sure the temperature in our upstairs bedroom was very close to this because ...

I was so excited about finding 12 acres of land we could actually afford that several features of the ~~crumbling~~ charming farmhouse were overlooked: When you turned on the bathroom tap, water leaked from the kitchen ceiling. Much of the electrical in the house had not been updated. And there wasn't ANY heat in the upstairs of our home.

January mornings were the most fun. I didn't have to worry about being groggy because as soon as I slid from underneath our warm covers, it was like being tossed into a bucket of ice. Every morning our family would dash out of bed and run like fools, elbowing each other to be the first down the stairs and into the slightly warmer part of our home.

By this time, I was so wide awake, I didn't even need coffee. (So if you look on the bright side, we were saving money on heat and hot beverages.)

We did have plans to install a woodstove to improve our situation. But it was costly and since we didn't own any forested land, "learning to install a woodstove and chop our own firewood" was scratched off our to-do list in favour of investing in skills that would save us money and bring us closer to that ultimate dream of living off the land.

So there were no cozy fires, no hand knit socks (my fibre skills had not yet advanced to this level) and instead of spending my evenings with a warm blanket and a cup of cider, we were shoveling mountains of snow from our 600-foot driveway set on the perfect slope so that as soon as you finished shoveling, the snow would blow right back in. (We later found out the previous owners parked at the end of the driveway and walked the 600 feet several times a day.) We have since remedied the driveway situation by changing its angle, but that first winter was a perfect storm.

Do you know what saved me from wallowing in an icy puddle of misery? This challenge. Because I had hope. Hope that someday we would be sitting on our front porch overlooking a thriving homestead and laughing about the struggles we went through our first year homesteading. Someday, I thought, this will be funny.

So despite the cold and our farmhouse troubles, I proudly made my first ball of lopsided mozzarella cheese while imagining myself milking my own dairy cow or goat. Much to my husband's dismay, I also saved money by making my own peppermint deodorant and forcing him to wear it to work.

And I spent my afternoons sifting through seed catalogs, dreaming of growing enough vegetables to feed our family for six months of the year. (This was despite the fact that my success as a gardener was limited to mostly killing plants and that I had yet to grow a bumper crop of anything except those things my family really didn't want to eat. Take cabbage and zucchini, for example.)

You will also find "learning to spin wool" in the list of skills for January. In reality, I spun in October a few weeks after the challenge was finished. Why? It was the only local course I could find and I felt it was important to learn from and meet other spinners. I've included it here because I wish I could have learned this skill in January instead of in the fall when I was busy harvesting, putting the garden to bed, and getting the farm ready for yet another winter.

Does this mean I didn't learn 52 homesteading skills in one year? No. I actually learned more. Take raising chicks, for example. I could have also added many other skills such as "learning to prevent and treat chicken mites," "how to keep eggs from freezing in the winter," or "fixing a cracked chicken beak."

It is almost impossible to take on any new homesteading activity without learning a thousand other skills. And as soon as you think 'I've got this,' Mother Nature laughs and throws you an unexpected frost, a hungry predator, or a swarm of bees. The learning never ends. And that's OK. Because life without challenge would be BORING.

Homesteading, as hard as it may be at times, will add excitement to your life … and chicken poop on your front step. I'm just saying.

Peppermint Deodorant

Mozzarella Cheese

Eating Only What You Grow

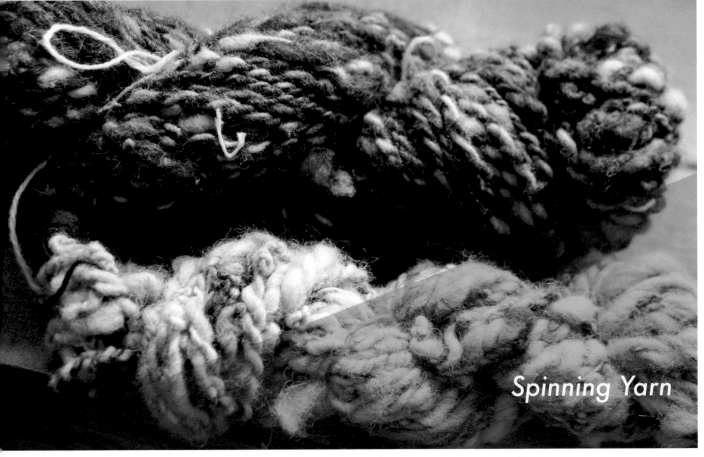

Spinning Yarn

project 1

cooling peppermint deodorant

I know what you're thinking. The first skill in this book is making deodorant? This is so lame and gross and frankly, Kimberlee, I think you're a little strange. OK, so maybe I did end up taking this homesteading thing too far, but hear me out.

The hardest part about homesteading is simply getting started. So start small. Making deodorant is easy. You can't fail at this. Your armpits will be happier, your bank account will be happier, and this one, tiny success will encourage you to move on to another. And that is how I learned 52 skills in one year. Wow, I made my own deodorant. Maybe I could try making cheese? Holy mozzarella, I did it! I wonder if I can preserve my own vegetables? And so on and so on and so on until before you know it, you've just blown yourself away by how much you accomplished in a year. So start your homesteading journey with deodorant or at least another easy project. But whatever you do, don't put down this book and let it grow dust. Pick a skill and go for it.

Why make your own deodorant? First, you can avoid all the chemicals, synthetic fragrances, and other questionable ingredients in most commercial varieties. So if you wanted to, you could even lick your armpits. Isn't that great?

Second, in my not so humble opinion, this simple recipe is even better than most of the pricey natural deodorants I previously bought at the store. I admit I had to force my husband to try it. I could hear him in the bathroom fretting about the deodorant staining his good work shirt and yes, there was also some muttering about his crazy wife. But if you ask him, he will grudgingly admit my homemade deodorant is actually pretty good. So go wild! Go crazy! And make some homemade deodorant.

ingredients

- 1 cup coconut oil
- 1 tbsp baking soda
- ¼ cup arrowroot starch
- ½ tbsp bentonite clay
- 10 drops tea tree oil and 10 drops peppermint oil (These are the oils I used, but feel free to experiment with your own combinations. My friend, for example, makes this recipe using doTERRA's Citrus Bliss, bergamot, and lemongrass essential oils.)

*Makes approximately three muffin tin sized deodorants.

1. Melt the oil over low heat.

2. Stir in the baking soda, starch, and clay, and mix until it reaches a smooth consistency. Add essential oils.

3. Pour into muffin tins or an old deodorant container. Let cool and store in the fridge.

TIP
To help unstick the deodorant from your pan, place the muffin tin in the freezer for a few minutes. Then, simply wedge a butter knife underneath the bars and they should easily pop out.

project 2

30-minute mozzarella cheese

Exhilarating. That's the best word I could come up with to describe how I felt holding my first homemade ball of lopsided cheese. Who knew making cheese could be just as thrilling as Disney's Expedition Everest roller coaster or zip lining in Costa Rica? Yes, my friends, cheese making should be listed as one of the most exhilarating experiences on earth.

Of course, my mozzarella was far from perfect, but it might as well have been. I was incredibly, immensely, positively proud of myself. Maybe it's because I secretly thought this was going to be a disaster or that cheese making should be left to the artisans — not overeager amateurs like myself with a very, VERY sketchy track record of success in the kitchen. But I did it. And you can too.

All it takes is 30 minutes and you could be holding your own ball of delicious cheese. You could eat it raw, grate it over pizza or just have your friends over for wine and cheese and oh-so-casually mention you made the mozzarella yourself. I know you want to, so let's get started.

ingredients

- ¼ rennet tablet
- 1¼ cup cool, chlorine-free water, divided
- 1½ tsp citric acid
- 4 L or 1 US gallon whole, organic cow's milk
- 2 tsp non-iodized salt

supplies

- Two small bowls
- Two large pots
- Slotted spoon (not plastic)
- Long knife
- Colander
- Digital thermometer
- Rubber gloves
- Large bowl of room-temperature water

1. In a small bowl, dissolve ¼ rennet tablet in ¼ cup of room-temperature water and set aside. Wrap and store the remainder of the tablet in the freezer.

2. In another small bowl, mix citric acid into remaining room temperature water. Stir until the citric acid is dissolved and pour the mixture into a large pot.

3. Add the milk to the pot with the citric acid and stir vigorously with a slotted spoon while slowly heating the milk to 90°F. This will cause the milk to curdle slightly.

4. Take your pot off the burner and slowly stir in the rennet mixture with an up-and-down motion of the slotted spoon for approximately 30 seconds or at least long enough to ensure the rennet makes its way to the bottom of your pot.

5. Cover the pot and let it sit undisturbed for 5 minutes. This is when things start to get exciting. There should now be a clear separation between the curd (solid) and the whey (liquid). If not, let it sit for a few more minutes.

6. Cut the curd in long sections with a knife that reaches to the bottom of the pot.

7. Put the pot back on the stove and continue to heat it to 110°F while stirring the curd with the slotted spoon.

8. Take the pot off the burner and you guessed it … stir, stir, stir some more (for about 2 to 5 minutes). **Note: The more you stir, the firmer the curds will become.**

9. Heat another large pot of water to 185°F.

10. Ladle the curds into a colander, folding them together toward the centre and draining the whey as you go.

11. Dip the colander containing the curds into the hot water and use the slotted spoon to fold the curds back into the centre of the colander until they reach 160 to 170°F.

12. Remove the curds from the colander, add salt and with your hands form it all into a ball while squeezing out any liquid. Start stretching. It will be hot so you will probably want to use gloves. Unfortunately, I could only find one glove so yes, my other hand in the bottom right picture is burning. Continue to stretch the curd, almost the same as kneading dough, until it is soft and shiny. The more you work the cheese, the firmer it will become. If the curds do not stretch easily, return them to the pot and reheat them to 160 to 170°F. Try stretching them again.

13. Form the cheese into one large ball or you can get fancy and braid it, make cheese strings or whatever your imagination can come up with.

14. Cool the cheese by submerging it in a bowl of room-temperature water for about 15 minutes. And ta da ... you have your own homemade mozzarella! You may now crank up the tunes and perform a little celebratory cheese dance. It's best fresh so don't party for too long before gobbling it all up. I mean ... dividing it equally among your family.

P.S. Don't throw away the leftover whey. You can use it to make ricotta cheese.

project 3

seeds and eating only what you grow

I read several times in many books that newbie gardeners should start small and slowly grow their garden in size. Of course, I didn't listen to this advice. I now had all this farm land to play with and I was embarking on a great homesteading quest. Why should I wait to expand?

So I announced to my 24 readers ... err, I mean millions and millions of fans, that as part of my challenge I was going to grow enough vegetables to feed my family for at least six months of the year.

Sounds completely reasonable, right?

You're going to be totally shocked when I tell you I failed. So I didn't acquire this skill and quickly gave up on the parts of the garden I couldn't manage.

So what can I, a gardening flop, possibly share with you about planning one? What not to do. Here is what I've learned from my favourite school — Hard Knocks. I just so happen to hold a Master's degree with honours.

10 tips for planning your first vegetable garden

Focus on what really matters

There are so many gardening books out there, you could spend your whole life reading them and never plant a single seed.

Sure, go ahead and read a couple books, take a course, watch a few videos, but an even better idea is to plant something. Novel idea, I know. Order some seeds, pick a sunny spot in your yard or balcony, apply a good dose of compost to the soil, and follow the directions on the seed packet.

It really is that easy. Plants don't want to die. You have to work as hard as me to kill them.

It's all about the soil

If I had spent more time concerned with what was in my soil than with what I was going to plant in the ground, I would have had better success.

You might make the mistake of thinking just because grass grows in your yard, vegetables will too. Wrong! I can confidently write that the success of your veggies will be directly related to the quality of your earth.

Now, the vegetables still might grow in poor soil, but they will most likely be stunted. How do I know? Because I tried simply removing the grass from our homestead and planting directly in the remaining soil. When my veggies didn't grow, I thought our garden was plagued with grubs until I finally realized — no, it was just our subpar soil.

Let there be light

If your vegetables had a choice, they would spend the majority of their time basking in full sun. Unfortunately, not everyone has a yard that receives at least six to eight hours of direct light. If yours happens to be shaded by trees, for example, all is not lost.

There are a few vegetables that even prefer, or will at least tolerate, partial shade including leafy greens of all kinds (lettuce, kale, spinach, and Swiss chard, for example) and radishes. If you have a corner that receives at least four to five hours of sun each day, you can also add some root vegetables like beets and carrots as well as beans and peas.

The closer, the better

Where should you place your garden? In your kitchen. Because when you're whipping up an omelette for breakfast and suddenly get a craving for parsley, the farther you have to walk, the less likely you will be to harvest it. Yes, I'm lazy! But trust me on this one. The closer your garden is, the more you will use it and the easier it will be to keep an eye on those weeds, which, unfortunately, grow much faster than the vegetables.

Now you may not be able to plant in your kitchen, but you can place your garden as close as possible to your front door. Of course, crops you don't harvest as often such as potatoes or corn could be planted farther out. But not too far away so as to discourage you from keeping a frequent eye on them. Weeds and hungry bugs will work tirelessly against you.

Grow what you love

It may seem like a good idea to try growing your own Brussels sprouts, but it won't be if your Brussels sprouts stay on the stalk and rot because it turns out Brussels sprouts really aren't your family's favourite. Just so you know our family has never done anything so wasteful — at least not more than a couple times. And I know how cool collards, kohlrabi, and fava beans sound, but think carefully about your family's reaction when they are staring at it on their dinner plate possibly for the sixth night in a row. Narrow it down to your favourites and you'll be happy you did.

Stick to the basic varieties

There are dozens of varieties of carrot and tomatoes seeds, for example. If you aren't careful, you can easily spend hundreds of your gardening dollars just on seeds. I ordered more than 80 seed packets and plants for my first garden. I'm not joking. I planted several varieties of every vegetable as well as everything from skirret and sea kale to soapwort (because I was, of course, going to dry the roots and make homemade soap. As you have likely guessed that never happened, but I had dreams … oh, so many dreams for that garden.)

I have since learned it is best for beginners to start with the basic varieties and branch out as both you and your garden grow.

Beware of seed catalogs

One of the best seed choosing tips I've ever received is from Alyson Chisholm of Windy Hill Organic Farm in McKees Mills, New Brunswick, during one of her gardening classes.

When you're perusing all of these enticing seed catalogs and trying to figure out which of the amazing vegetables you should grow (because they will all sound amazing), read between the lines. For example, if the catalog describes a cucumber as vigorous with excellent disease resistance, but doesn't mention anything about its taste, there is a good chance it lacks flavour. And if the catalog raves about its exceptional taste and beautiful colouring, but doesn't refer to its disease tolerance, it's most likely not.

What this means is you have to decide what's most important to you. For me, it's taste. I will choose the tastiest variety over disease resistance, early maturing, high yielding … hmmm, maybe this is why many of my vegetables fail to thrive.

Companion or confusion planting?

I love the idea of pairing different vegetables and flowers together to confuse garden pests. Unfortunately, companion planting, as it's called, also confused ME.

I had so many different plants and varieties scattered around the garden that I could no longer remember what was where. It was also time consuming.

I remember my parents offering to keep the kids busy one afternoon while I planted. When they returned hours later they were surprised to see I was still working in the same vegetable bed.

I explained I had just read a book on companion planting and so I was spending hours planting one onion bulb next to one carrot seed followed by one beet seed. I did that by hand over and over and over again. I had planned two such 8-foot beds. I felt so smart outwitting those bugs. No way would the carrot rust fly be able to find my carrots hidden amongst these other vegetables. Muhahaha.

I gave up after the first 8 feet. I literally threw the rest of the carrot seeds into the other bed. I was done in seconds. And you know what? The carrots in both gardens did equally well. I did have to thin the second bed, but it was much less time consuming than planting all those individual seeds by hand.

I am not saying companion planting doesn't work (because I really don't know) or that you shouldn't do it (hey, it may be worth a try). I am saying you can't get hung up on the details — especially when you're starting out. Plant first. You can find friends for your vegetables later.

Help — There's no shame in it

I used MOTHER EARTH NEWS' online vegetable garden planner to design my first beds. With just a few clicks I could map out my space, plug in the vegetables I wanted to grow, and the program took care of the rest.

It creates a list of when I should start my seeds indoors, when I should transplant, and when I should plant outdoors. It figures out my spacing and crop rotation. The only thing it doesn't do is plant my garden, which is really too bad. I'll have to talk to them about adding this feature.

There is even a space to write notes such as when you were able to harvest those first tomatoes, which squash varieties performed best, or interesting garden ideas you came across elsewhere. Unfortunately, I didn't remember to use this feature, but I wish I had, as I now uselessly try to recall these details.

I know I could just use grid paper and follow the directions on the back of the seed packets to plan my garden and maybe someday that's what I'll do. But for a beginner like myself, this program was worth the small investment. Two green thumbs up!

Let it go, let it go, let it gooooooo

Your first garden is not going to be perfect.

It will rain too frequently or there will be a drought. Potato bugs will chow down on your prized purple spuds and you will have to arm yourself with a vacuum and suck those pests up. (See, another reason to ensure your garden is planted as close to your home as possible. You never know when you might need to plug in a vacuum). Or you'll find yourself crying over a surprise frost that froze the tomatoes you were going to preserve for the winter.

This is all part of the fun. No, really. If gardening was easy, you wouldn't feel that deep satisfaction at the end of the season when you celebrate the vegetables that did well. Yes, there will be some! So take a deep breath and enjoy the challenge. Someday you'll have aesthetic pea gravel in your paths, perfectly mulched beds and you will finally be able to grow cucumbers. Maybe.

project 4

spinning yarn

You might think taking a few days off to learn how to spin wool would be a relaxing activity. You would be wrong!

I wasn't even halfway through the beginner class and I was already having visions of violently chucking my spinning wheel out the window.

I had traveled three hours with my mom to St. Andrews, N.B., to spend two days learning how to spin wool with expert hand spinner Rachel Dalton of Brigadoon Fiber and Alpaca Farm in Hoyt, N.B.

I had visions of sipping tea while laughing with the other women in the group as we leisurely spun wool in our bare feet. A few minutes into the class and I was already working up a sweat pumping the single treadle (the pedal that turns the wheel) with one or both feet as if my life depended on it.

I might as well have hit the gym for the more modern version of a spinning class. Was I out of shape? I wondered as I looked around the room and saw no one else struggling. I was sure my wheel was broken or maybe needed greasing.

One of the other women in the class, likely out of pity, offered to switch wheels. She had a double treadle (two pedals) and for some reason this made all the difference. I could finally relax and get into a rhythm focusing on what really mattered — spinning the wool (not that this was any easier).

Secretly, I was hoping to see my kind rescuer struggle with the single treadle so I wouldn't feel so bad about my own incompetence. But alas, no. To my humiliation, she actually preferred it.

And this is why I'm going to recommend to anyone who wants to learn how to spin, to take a class where you can try different spinning wheels, where you can talk to the instructor to figure out why your wheel keeps turning backwards when it's not supposed to, or why your yarn keeps twisting.

Despite the many problems I encountered, 15 hours of practice later and lots of help from Rachel, I managed to make something that at least looked like yarn. I'd say it is the most unique yarn in all the land. Can I knit with it? Ahhhh ... maybe.

Since this was my first attempt at spinning and I'm still learning myself, I asked Rachel, who has been spinning since she was 12 years old, to provide some tips for us newbies. Her tips follow:

Be creative and stay calm

The image you have of calmly sitting on the porch effortlessly spinning while listening to the soft *whhhrrrr* of the wheel will come to be. Spinning looks effortless once everything is coordinating, but the road to finding your rhythm can be bumpy.

Test out different wheels

This might seem obvious, or to those without access to a spinning store — impossible. Yet it's SO important. Not every wheel is made the same and there are so many variations to something as simple as 'the wheel'. A good spinning shop or guild will accommodate you (and maybe offer tea!) while you test. Single or double treadles, large or small flyers, wooden or metal wheels. They are as unique as the spinners who use them.

If you simply are not able to visit a spinning store, research the different wheels and stick to the well-known manufacturers (you get what you pay for) and read the buyers' reviews carefully. Most of the reviewers are experienced spinners whose opinions can certainly help. Be prepared to invest in a quality machine that will last for years, if not a lifetime.

Don't splurge on antiques for your learner's wheel

Antique wheels often need pieces rebuilt, have seized or missing pieces, or are simply more than a beginner might know how to handle. Instead, display that gorgeous piece in a corner in your home and find a sturdy and serviceable modern wheel to start playing with.

Sit and treadle

This might sound silly, but pushing your foot up and down is not fool proof. Working in tandem with the footman (the bar that connects the treadle to the fly wheel and causes it to turn) and the wheel to keep it spinning not only at a steady pace, but in the right direction, can be challenging.

Attempt different speeds

This is a skill that will come in handy when spinning different weight yarns and plying (spinning two individual threads together). Treadling while watching TV, reading a book, or chatting on the phone helps build muscle memory that will pay off when you add the fibre.

Start with undyed top or roving

We're drawn to colour, sparkle, and shine. But in all of my beginner classes I have my students learn to spin using natural, undyed top (fibres hand combed into the same direction with little air between them) or roving (wool that has been run through a mill on a carding machine; fibres may not all run in the same direction creating a fuzzier texture).

The dying process can change the way a fibre drafts (separates into smaller sections). Using a natural roving mitigates this and allows you to focus on the fibre and making a continuous thread, rather than neps (small entanglements or knots of fibres) or felted areas.

Take one skill at a time

As much as I love working from the ground up on my own fleeces, take it one skill at a time. Spend a little extra and purchase prepped top (fibre that has already been cleaned and combed). It can make the learning process so much smoother for your first initial foray into the craft.

Pre-draft

Drafting is the act of separating a piece of roving or top into smaller portions that can then be more easily fed onto the bobbin.

Watch videos on drafting and find a technique that you're comfortable with. Play with your fibre and become intimate with how it pulls apart and drafts. As a seasoned spinner,

I pre-draft fibre if it's not one I've used before or from a new supplier. Even within our herd of alpaca, different animal's fibre acts differently.

Pre-drafting also means less to worry about as you're spinning it into yarn. Thicker pieces of roving will require more coordination and muscle memory in your hands to achieve the correct thickness of thread. Pre-drafting will prevent an over twisted or under twisted yarn from entering and tangling it into an unmanageable portion.

Keep your first piece

No matter how bumpy, overspun, or poky it may be, frame your first yarn and put it in a place of honour. It will be a great reminder of how far you've come. Mine is a yellow Suffolk I made on a drop spindle when I was 12. I drag it out to show all my students and it has a place of honour in our farm shop.

Have fun and be persistent

Don't worry. It will all fall into place and you'll be creating beautiful, one-of-a-kind yarns in no time. But don't think you'll ever stop learning. There never seems to be an end to the new techniques, colours, or fibres you can explore.

Learning to spin can be both gratifying and challenging. Hopefully with these few tips, you can avert many of the mistakes I made as a new spinner.

FEBRUARY

My life is embarrassing. I came to this conclusion during a recent doctor's visit. It was time to put my coat back on — only the zipper was broken. Instead of fixing it, I had just been leaving it zipped at the end so I could step in and out of my coat as needed. Simple solution, right?

Well, it had seemed like a good idea until I had to perform this feat in public. I tried to be 'oh so cool and casual' as I jumped into my coat and yanked it up over my shoulders all the while hoping my doctor could see the practicality in this time-saving although tricky maneuver. Alas, I don't think she did. I'm pretty sure she just thought I was weird.

Unfortunately, this month's embarrassments didn't end there.

We had to install a new metal roof on our farmhouse. The old one was starting to grow moss, and we were running out of buckets to catch the leaks.

The day before the roofers arrived, a horrible thought occurred to me — they're going to be able to see into each and every one of my windows ... into this mess I call my life.

We had garbage bags on window ledges where we had begun to strip paint. We had a hole in the floor where we started to wire a dining room light. We had a giant pipe floating along the entrance wall because we were in the midst of fixing an improperly vented dryer. The playroom (who am I kidding? I really mean my whole house) looked like a large tribe of monkeys recently took up residence and scattered laundry and toys everywhere.

So why didn't I just close the blinds? Because I hadn't taken the time to put them up. Don't worry. There weren't any windows in the bathroom — at least not in the downstairs one.

This is my real life.

You can't see the floor in my car, I haven't dusted since we moved in, and my sink is almost always full of dishes.

You may be impressed by the fact that I have time to work on all these homesteading projects with two kids in the house, a husband who works full time, and farm renovations to complete, but the truth is ... I couldn't and I still can't do it all. Shocking, right?

I wish I was a 'homestead star.' (You know, like rock star or movie star. What? You don't think it's the same thing?) but just like everyone else, I only have 24 hours each day and I have to choose how to spend those hours.

And just like everyone else who takes on a new project, I had to give up doing something else in return. So instead of watching TV, or religiously mopping and vacuuming my floors, dusting my shelves, and organizing my closets, this month I made my own laundry detergent and dish soap, started seeds indoors, and learned how to convert a cow stall to a chicken coop.

And that's OK because we're living our homesteading dreams! Our dream just happens to also include broken zippers, dirty dishes, and holes in our floor. I'm sure this is exactly what your dreams look like too, right?

Cow Stall to Chicken Coop

Homemade Laundry Soap

All Natural Dish Soap

Starting Seeds Indoors

project 5

cow stall to chicken coop

Sundown. Three years earlier. I grabbed my flashlight in a panic and ran outside. It was dark and I had yet to do the nightly chicken round-up at our former house. I know what you're thinking. Don't chickens march all by themselves into their coop at night?

That is what they are supposed to do. Unfortunately, not all of our chickens could agree on this simple protocol. Some of our very special chickens decided one night that it would be much more fun to sleep high in the trees and then have a good clucking laugh as they watched me try and capture them all in my pajamas. Oh, the fun we had with our former chickens who refused to roost in their coop.

I don't know if this stuff happens to real farmers who know better than to let chickens "free range" or who at least know to clip their chickens' wings so they can't get up to such silly antics, but at the time I thought this was a cruel practice.

Actually, I still have a hard time doing this, but at least now I understand why it is done. Chickens can fly — very high. So high that some nights I couldn't reach my feathered friends who would then become raccoon dinner. As you can probably guess, we didn't have these chickens (given to us by a local farmer who wanted to downsize his flock) for very long and that's why "learning to raise chicks" is included as part of this homesteading challenge.

Now you're probably wondering why I am recounting this story. This month our friends' home had burned to the ground and they needed a temporary place to house their animals. They had lost everything except what was most important — their children and livestock.

Although our dairy barn (actually two barns spanning a length of 200 feet) is huge, it was not set up for any animals other than cows. So we had to come up with a quick and easy solution to convert an existing stall into a functional and safe home for both their chickens and two, oh-so-very-cute miniature donkeys.

Roosts

One important item our stalls did not have were roosts. Surprisingly, the chickens were not fazed by the lack of traditional sleeping arrangements. They took matters into their own chicken feet and roosted along the old feeding troughs. Bonus — the poop goes into the trough making clean-up a little easier. But if your structure does not have a feeding trough, you can simply install 2X4's or tree branches which, as you may have guessed, are perfectly shaped for bird feet. It is recommended to allow a minimum of 8 inches roosting space per hen.

Predator proofing

Our No. 1 concern was not roosts, but predators. Our first attempt at chicken keeping was thwarted by a sneaky ferret who burrowed underneath our coop and squeezed in through a small opening — killing all of the remaining birds that weren't previously eaten by the raccoon. So it goes without saying — we don't want this to ever happen again.

So the most important task was to extend the walls of our stalls to the ceiling to deter large predators. We used 2-inch dog pen fencing because that's what we had on hand, but if you are buying new supplies, go with

½ inch by ½ inch, 16-gauge galvanized, welded wire mesh. We then wrapped the 2-inch wire with ¼ inch welded wire mesh to prevent smaller predators like rats from getting in. Yes, even rats love chicken dinner.

The stall floors were cement so we didn't have to worry about any hungry animals burrowing up through the soil. But if you have a dirt floor, it is suggested to bury wire mesh 12 to 18 inches under the ground.

Truth be told, I doubt any animal would actually try to break into the converted coop thanks to the chickens' BFFs — Rosie and Daisy, the two miniature donkeys who share the same space. Donkeys are natural guard animals who don't take kindly to intruders — unless, of course, you are human and happen to be holding treats.

Cleaning up

If you've ever kept chickens, you know they poop a lot and they will poop anywhere and everywhere. So we covered the cement floor with absorbent pine shavings, which neutralize any nasty odors. Eventually the bedding and other matter will end up in the compost and a new layer added.

Nest boxes

Our neighbours came up with a creative and inexpensive method for building nesting boxes using plastic pails set on their side and filled with a cozy layer of pine shavings.

Traditionally, nesting boxes are built out of wood and secured to the wall in a row. Our boxes are 12 square inches and because we have 30 chickens, we have nine of them. You will need roughly one nesting box per three or four hens.

The nesting boxes can be set wherever you like as long as they're lower than your roosts so the chickens don't decide to sleep (and poop!) in their nesting boxes. It goes without saying — you want your eggs to be clean.

Waterers and feeders

We use a bucket for water and bowls for our chickens' food, but this was a mistake. In less than five minutes, the chickens dirty their water and food with bedding. Instead, we're planning to mount our feeders and waterers on the wall or hang them from the ceiling. And that's it. Just a million, time consuming, easy steps and you will have a cozy home for your flock.

project 6
homemade laundry soap

I'll bet making your own laundry soap was at the top of your list of dream homesteading skills to learn, right? What? It wasn't? Oh, you are missing out on some serious fun, my friend. And an annual savings of $87.03. Wait! Don't go!

I admit that doesn't sound impressive, but I can whip up a batch of this soap in minutes and it lasts me six months. So if I made this recipe twice a year, I would still only be spending about 30 minutes a year making soap. Where else can you earn $87.03 for just half an hour of your time? Now that's what I call a good deal.

The savings

So let's say you do eight loads of laundry a week. I know what you're thinking. How wasteful! Eight loads? I'm blaming the kids, my husband, the chickens, and the mud. I don't know what is wrong with my family but they are constantly spilling things, covering themselves in dirt, and leaving towels and clothes on the floor so that it feels like I'm changing the kids' shirts and picking up laundry every 10 minutes.

I, on the other hand, am not nearly so careless. I like to wear the same pants all week long and only wash my tops when the armpits start to stink. Aren't you impressed? Ahem. OK, back to our calculations. My so-called "green" laundry detergent costs me $11 for 50 loads. In comparison, my homemade laundry soap costs about 54¢ per 50 loads. (That's just one cent a load!) If you do eight loads a week, that's 416 loads a year, which works out to $91.52 in store-bought detergent or $4.49 in homemade laundry soap.

Which one are you going to choose? That was a rhetorical question. Of course, you're going to make your own. By the end of the year that money will buy you more than a dozen of those cute fluffy chicks you've been dreaming about or heirloom seeds for your garden or how about your first package of bees? And I know this is going to be hard to believe but ... get ready to jump up and down because the excitement doesn't end here.

You will save the world! Or maybe just your own backyard from otherwise nasty, polluting chemicals. I could go on, but I'm sure you are just itching to get started so ...

supplies

- 4 liters of water
- ½ bar of pure castile soap, grated
- ½ cup washing soda
- ¼ cup borax

1. In a large pot, mix water and grated soap over medium heat until soap is completely dissolved.

2. Add washing soda and borax and mix well.

3. Use a funnel to pour the contents into your jars. Give it another stir and let sit for 24 hours. You'll know it's ready when it has turned into a gel-like substance. Over time it will separate slightly. Don't worry. It will all dissolve in the washing machine. I use one tablespoon per load.

See, wasn't that easy? I bet you can't wait to wash your next load of laundry. This soap is going to make cleaning your stinky socks and underwear so much more fun.

A DIRTY LITTLE SECRET

You may not need to use laundry detergent or soap to get your clothes clean, according to Jeffrey Hollender, co-founder and former CEO of Seventh Generation, a well-known company that sells green cleaning products among other items. In an article in *The Wall Street Journal,* he is quoted as saying: "You don't even need soap to wash most loads. The agitation of washing machines often does the job on its own."

So there you have it. You may not even need to go through the trouble of making your own laundry soap. Simply pre-treat tough stains and then throw your clothes in the wash. It doesn't get any greener or cheaper than that. Unless you want to buy a washboard and hand scrub your laundry. Anyone?

green cleaning tips

Concerned about soap build-up?
Once a month, run a load with a cup of vinegar or use vinegar in your washing machine's rinse cycle. BONUS — Vinegar will help fight static cling.

Want whiter whites?
Add lemon juice to your white load and then, if possible, hang your laundry to dry in the sun.

Clothes smelling stinky?
Try adding a couple drops of tea tree oil, which is both antifungal and antibacterial, to your wash.

Ditch the fabric softener
Washing with soap automatically leaves laundry softer to the touch.

project 7
all natural dish soap

If you thought making your own detergent was exciting, wait until you try making dish soap. Insert nerdy homesteader laugh here. I think my detergent works well, but this Sal Suds based dish washing detergent? It's AMAZING.

The first castile dish soap I shared on my blog did not suds up. The recipe I have included here is a revised version that involves whipping the soap in a blender to get an even consistency and a little extra suds. But to be completely honest, I have discovered a better and simpler solution — Dr. Bronner's Sal Suds. Unlike the castile soap, Sal Suds is a detergent BUT it's not made from petro-chemicals. It uses plant-based surfactants. Even the Environmental Working Group (EWG) gives it an A rating, which means there are few or no known or suspected hazards to health or the environment.

Sal Suds is a completely natural, biodegradable cleaner that creates bubbles, cuts grease, and smells like you just entered a pine forest. So while you're doing dishes, you can pretend you're enjoying a leisurely walk in the forest and not slaving over three days of dirty plates. What I also love about Sal Suds is that unlike castile soap, you can combine it with vinegar for spot-free dishes and streak-free glasses.

Unfortunately, it's more expensive than my original recipe. In fact, you may only be saving a few cents, so if you're not obsessed with bubbles, you may want to try the castile soap recipe instead. In this case, you'll save $4 in less than the time it takes to actually do your dishes. A bottle of natural dish soap is about $5 at the store and a similar sized container of this homemade soap is about $1.

You will notice I have added vegetable glycerin to both recipes. This is to prevent "dishpan hands." The glycerin helps keep my skin soft while hand-washing dishes. No matter which recipe you choose, you will save your money, protect our planet from nasty chemicals, and get your dishes squeaky clean. So let's get to it.

Option 1 - Sal Suds Dish Washing Detergent

1. Mix the warm water and salt together until the salt has completely dissolved. Note: The salt is what will thicken your soap. If you omit the salt, your solution will be watery.

2. In a separate bowl, combine the Sal Suds and vinegar.

3. Stir the Sal Suds and vinegar mixture into the salt water and continue stirring until thickened. Mix in the vegetable glycerin.

The soap will store well in your favourite dish soap container for about a month.

ingredients

- ½ cup warm, distilled water
- 2 tsp kosher salt
- ½ cup Sal Suds
- ½ cup distilled, white vinegar
- 1 tbsp vegetable glycerin

* This recipe is adapted from thehippyhomemaker.com

Option 2 - Castile Whipped Dish Soap

1. In a saucepan, mix the water and grated soap over medium heat until the soap is completely dissolved.

2. Add washing soda and mix well.

3. Remove from heat and let cool. Stir in the vegetable glycerin.

4. Let sit overnight.

5. In the morning, the mixture should be very thick. Pour into your blender and mix until frothy on a low speed for about 15 seconds. Store your soap in a covered bowl or another container with a wide mouth. Use a spoon to add a scoop to your dish water.

6. To ensure the castile soap and washing soda do not leave a residue on your dishes, use a couple tablespoons of vinegar in your rinse water.

ingredients

- 1¼ cups water
- 0.9 oz (about ½ cup) castile bar soap, grated
- 1 tbsp washing soda
- 1 tbsp vegetable glycerin
- Vinegar for rinsing

NOTE
The washing soda in this recipe is used to help remove grease and stains, but it may cause aluminum to pit and change colour. Don't wash your aluminum pots and pans with this soap.

bonus skill

starting seeds indoors

I can do magic. And you thought my biggest talent was homesteading. Pshhh ... I have the power to transform small, insignificant kernels into the tastiest, freshest, most delicious tomatoes you've ever eaten. What? That's not magic, you say?

Then you haven't planted a tiny seed in soil and watched as it slowly pushes through the ground shooting its way towards the sun, dancing and wiggling as it proudly bursts open to reveal its first leaves. Amazingly, that one tiny seedling will eventually transform itself into pounds of irresistible tomatoes.

This is magic. And you don't even have to attend a single Hogwarts' Herbology class. You can easily perform your own incantations at home simply by starting your seeds indoors. Now, Kimberlee. Why would I bother doing this when I can just buy transplants at the store? First, one plant is roughly the same price as a whole package of seeds. Second, you won't have the same selection or varieties at the garden store as you can find in the seed catalogs. Third, watching your seeds magically turn into vegetables is a life changing experience you don't want to skip out on.

supplies

Containers

Your local garden store will likely sell seed starting trays, which work great, but you can also reuse any old plastic container including milk jugs, water bottles, or margarine tubs. We saved yogurt containers for years and these are the perfect planters to start larger vegetables like tomatoes, peppers, pumpkins, and squash. Punch a few small holes in the bottom of your container and place the lid underneath to catch any runoff. This prevents your soil from staying damp and growing mould.

Seed-starting trays often include clear plastic domes, which keep your seedlings and soil moist to improve germination. If you're using your own containers and want a dome, you can use a plastic bag instead.

Soil

Some gardeners enjoy making their own seed-starting mix. But beware. You might make the mistake of thinking you can use earth from your backyard. And you can — if you don't mind oohing and ahhing over weeds. Yes, I did this. I was so excited to see what I thought was my first little pepper plant emerging from the soil when in fact it was just a weed. What I didn't realize was that outdoor soil is full of weeds and doesn't drain well.

So if you do want to make your own seed-starting mix, try a combination such as one third coco peat, one third vermiculite, or sand and one third weed-free compost. Or you can wimp out like me and buy a bag of seed-starting mix from the store. Once your seeds develop their first leaves, consider adding some worm castings to ensure you little seedlings continue to have enough nutrients to grow.

Water

This may be the hardest part about starting your seeds indoors. It sounds easy, but remembering to water your seedlings is tougher than you might think. I tend to let them dry out and then douse them with a jug of water and wonder why they aren't thriving. Don't do this. Grab a spray bottle and mist your seedlings every day or two to keep them moist.

Light

If your seedlings do not receive enough light, they will grow long, thin, and weak. These plants will have a difficult time adapting to the harsh and windy reality of the outdoors. Your best bet is to grow your seedlings in a south-facing window or purchase artificial lights. You don't need special, full-spectrum, grow lights, which can cost hundreds of dollars, to start your seeds indoors. We simply use an LED 4,000 K shop light. Keep your seedlings a few inches from the light for 8 to 10 hours a day.

Heat

Most seedlings will be happy to grow at room temperature although there are a few vegetables such as peppers that prefer extra warm soil to germinate. You can use a seedling heat mat to keep them cozy until they get their second set of true leaves.

Follow the directions on the seed packet

This is the easy part. The packet will tell you exactly how deep to plant your seed and how long it takes for the seeds to germinate, making it easy to calculate when the big day will arrive — the day you bring your troops out to battle in the real world — and hope they survive.

Note: It is recommended you "harden them off" first, which simply means placing them outside for a few hours a day out of direct sun and wind. You then slowly increase the amount of time they're outside by a couple hours each day. I admit this is a lot of work. I skipped this step and just planted them outside on a mild, cloudy day and then covered them with row covers if the weather station was calling for exceptionally windy or sunny conditions.

Of course, before you can plant your seeds, you need to order them. So if you haven't already, you may now excitedly rip open all the seed catalogs and enjoy heated debates among your family members over which mouth-watering selections to choose. Just try and keep your order to a reasonable size and then let the spring planting begin!

FYI

This is a bonus skill because I had already tried starting my seeds indoors before beginning this challenge. I wanted to include it here because I have so many other gardening skills in this book and I felt this one was too important not to be mentioned. So there are actually 53 skills you can learn in this book. Aren't you excited? My publishers were too when I surprised them with this extra skill.

MARCH

The bees are coming … I can hear their fragile wings beating and buzzing endlessly in my head. It sounds something like this: "You are a complete fool. You know nothing about bees and yet you have the audacity to order not one, but two hives? Be forewarned: You will be held responsible for our deaths." It turns out bees are kinda mean.

With two kids in the house, it is not uncommon for me to wake in the middle of the night, but lately I have been waking in fear. I toss and turn as I wonder how many bees are going to find their way up my pants, how I am going to summon the courage to stick my hand into a hive full of bees, and how I'm going to keep them from swarming our neighbours. And then I wonder … Why the heck am I doing this? Why can't I just get a dog or a cat?

Ah yes, because bees are extremely fascinating. My love affair with bees started way back in the seventh grade during the annual speech competition. While other kids spoke about hockey, pop stars, and summer vacations, I enthusiastically roused my classmates to all the wonders of bees. By the time I was done, I'm sure every one of them wanted their own pet hive.

Or maybe not. But I must have impressed the teacher because the bees and I won. Mostly because ... bees are intriguing.

Did you know there are guard bees stationed at the hive entrance on the alert to attack any intruders? There are also scout bees who search for new food sources and undertakers whose job it is to remove dead bees from the hive. There are even nannies who feed and care for the young.

Not only do each of the bees hold many of these jobs throughout their short lifetimes, they're also capable of remembering colours, landmarks, and even human faces. This is a handy fact to know when I go to steal some of their honey. Now you know the real reason it is so important to wear those bee veils — camouflage. I may have to think about getting a series of different masks.

Still not impressed? Bees have their own complex language. For example, through interpretive figure-8 movements called the "waggle dance," scout bees can report the distance and direction of food sources over 3 miles away.

Of course, bees are best known as pollinators. Without these essential creatures, more than a hundred thousand varieties of plants would disappear along with about half of the food in the grocery stores and that gorgeous, golden, sweet nectar we call honey.

So between my dreams of being stung, I dream of slurping honey and opening my own Etsy shop where I will sell all things bee related — soaps, candles, lip balm, honey hair conditioner .... Hey! Don't judge. You never know. Honey hair conditioner could become my top seller. My hypothetical Etsy shop may or may not be profitable, but that's not the point. The point is beekeeping could be fun ... and scary.

So I prayed to God every night asking Him to please let me not kill the bees. Please don't let them swarm anyone. And please, oh please don't let too many bees sting me. And then I read. And I mean I read. I read so much I think about giving up my challenge because I have too much to learn. I think I must have read every beekeeping book the library owns. And yet ... the only thing about beekeeping I was sure of was that it is learned through hands-on experience. So with much trepidation and a fervent hope that I will somehow find myself an experienced bee mentor, I ordered two nucs.

If you would have asked me before I started beekeeping what a nuc was, I would have told you it stood for nuclear missiles, but no, this is what you call a small honeybee colony created from a larger one.

After placing my order, I spent days and days and days not only practicing skills such as using a smoker, but debating which equipment to purchase. It was an exhausting and painful process because there were several choices and I really wanted to make the best one not only for me, but for my little bee friends (You hear that bees? I am trying to be your friend), which brings us to the first skill of this month ....

Build a Beehive

Light a Smoker

'Success'ion Planting

Crop Rotation and Controlling Pests

project 8
build a beehive

If you've ever traveled to a foreign country and found yourself struggling to understand the language, you know how it feels to enter the mysterious land of beekeeping.

I remember joining our local beekeeping association (you should do this too, by the way) and attending my first meeting. My hands were sweating even before I got out of the car. I felt like an intruder. Who did I think I was? I didn't belong among the commercial keepers who managed hundreds of hives. But I was determined to learn, and what better way than from local experts dealing with the same climate?

It turns out my fears were unfounded. Not only were they welcoming, but there were a few other newbies like myself who didn't even yet own a hive.

Unfortunately, I didn't actually learn much during my first meeting other than I needed to learn a lot more. Although I was listening during the presentation and they were obviously talking, I was unfamiliar with many of the terms. If this happens to you, don't get discouraged. Once you understand the language, it won't be long before you're casually throwing around terms like entrance reducers, bottom boards, and supers.

So with this in mind, it may not surprise you that just like everything else in beekeeping, the parts of a hive all come with strange names. And every beekeeper will likely have a slightly different setup depending on their climate, their needs, and their preferences.

I chose the most common type of hive, the Langstroth, with a few modifications. Let's start from the bottom up shall we?

Hive Stand

This one's simple. You need to keep your hives off the ground. Why? It helps prevent brush and snow from blocking the entrance, prevents rain from splashing into the hive, and raises the hive away from ground level moisture. A stand also helps prevent insects, rodents, and honey loving predators from making their way into the hive. Many sneaky animals will travel miles to get a mouthful of golden nectar or your bees. That's right. A skunk, for example, will visit your apiary at night and scratch the hive. When the bees come out to investigate, it simply grabs a bee, rolls it on the ground, and pops it in its mouth like a tasty honey-centred bonbon.

As interesting as this may be to witness, don't sacrifice your bees. Find a way to get your bees 18 to 24 inches off the ground. I've seen beekeepers use old pallets, concrete blocks, or you can simply build a stand like the one in the picture above.

Bottom Board

The name says it all. But like I warned you earlier, nothing is simple. There are two choices, of course — solid or screened. I chose the screened version. Why? It comes with a removable insert, which you can coat with a sticky substance such as cooking spray. The sticky board allows you to estimate the number of vampires (varroa mites), tick-sized parasites that feed on bee blood, in the hive.

The mites are small enough to fall through the wire mesh bottom as the bees clean the hive and groom each other. The troublesome insects then get stuck on the insert allowing you to count them. Too many and you will have to fight back with some kind of treatment or risk losing your hive.

Entrance Reducer

You'll definitely want to buy or make a few of these to use as your colony grows. When you first bring home your nuc (starter colony), you'll have about 10,000 bees and a couple frames of brood. By decreasing the size of the entrance, the bees will have an easier time defending their hive from other insects or rodents, who wouldn't mind an easy snack, until their numbers increase. If all goes well, you could have 65,000 to 80,000 bees come late summer.

Remember to remove your entrance reducer once nectar is plentiful or you will have many angry bees all struggling to find a way inside the hive.

You'll also want to use an entrance reducer in the winter to keep the hive warmer, prevent snow from blowing in, and discourage rodents from entering. If you aren't fast enough installing one, like me, those clever bees will make their own entrance reducer and fill the area with propolis.

Slatted Rack

If you want to be a really cool beekeeping rebel like me, grab yourself a slatted rack. This is not a well-known piece of equipment or one that is even widely used, but I think it's one of the best kept beekeeping secrets.

The rack is placed on top of your bottom board, which means your entrance is now farther away from your brood box, which is where the Queen lays her eggs and raises young bees (brood). This dead air space between your bottom board and brood box helps keep the bees cooler in the summer.

If you haven't noticed already, I'm a bit strange and so it may not surprise you that sometimes I will lay my head directly underneath my hives so I can have a look through the screen to see what fascinating things my bees are up to without having to open the hive and disturb the bees. (I heard that. My face is not disturbing.)

And as I hear them buzzing, I'm sure they're telling me how much they love the slatted rack. On hot days they have plenty of room to hang out along the rack fanning cool air into the hive instead of congesting the brood chamber.

Surprisingly, the Queen lays her eggs all the way to the bottom of the frames using a slatted rack. Most likely because her babies are farther away from the drafty entrance. Win! Win! Win!

I can't see into the hive during winter, but they are likely warmer thanks to the slatted rack. The extra air space will act as an insulating layer between the cool bottom and the brood box.

Brood boxes and supers

If you thought slatted racks were exciting, wait until you read this trick. The main part of your bee's home is made of boxes (the boxes containing baby bees are called "brood boxes" and the boxes containing honey are named supers because well, boxes of honey are pretty super, don't you think?).

There are three different sizes — deep, medium and shallow. Most beekeepers use the largest (a deep) for brood and mediums or shallows for honey. But this poses a challenge when you want to transfer a frame from a deep box into a medium or vice versa.

By using all medium boxes, you don't ever have to worry about this problem. Frames of brood and honey can easily be moved between boxes, which makes this system ideal when the time comes to split hives (making a second bee colony from your existing hive usually to prevent swarming). Another benefit of using all medium boxes is they are lighter (between 40 and 50 pounds as opposed to 79 and 90 pounds for 10-frame deep supers).

If you live in a cold climate like myself, you may also want to consider using what's called 8-frame equipment. A typical super can fit 10 frames, but you can also buy narrower supers that house 8 frames. I was first encouraged by my mentor (yes, I found one!), George Wheatley of Doré Products in New Brunswick, who has been keeping bees for 40 years. He told me his bees actually fare better over the winter in an 8-frame versus a 10-frame.

Why? I have heard from beekeepers that it's not uncommon for bees overwintering in 10-frames to starve even though there is still honey in the last two outer frames. And even if there is a second box stacked on top, the bees often opt to move up before consuming those last two frames of honey. It seems the poor bees can't break out of their warm cluster to reach their food. The narrower 8-frame equipment is better sized to the overwintering cluster of bees making it easier for them to keep warm.

Frames

Frames hold the honeycomb or brood comb and fit inside your brood box and supers. Most have a thin sheet of plastic or wax in the center, which the bees build their comb onto. These frames are put in what's called an extractor, which removes the honey without destroying the comb.

Tip: Don't invest in an extractor your first year. Your bees likely won't produce enough honey and I'm told many colonies won't make it through their first winter. Wait to buy an extractor until you need one or share with another beekeeper. You can also buy foundationless frames if you don't want to invest in an extractor or prefer to enjoy your honey still in the comb.

As a beginner, I was encouraged by George to start with plastic foundation and, although they were coated with wax, I gave them a second coat by melting beeswax and brushing it onto the frames. Why? The bees will be able to draw out the comb much faster, which means your colony will also be making honey sooner.

Warre Hive Roof and Quilt Box

When searching for a hive, I also considered the Warre. One of the aspects I loved about this hive is the roof, which is likely built similar to the one on your own home.

First, there is what's called a quilt box (basically a box filled with wood shavings) that sits on top of the hive. This acts just like the insulation in your attic — not only insulating, but preventing moisture from building up in the hive. The bottom of the quilt box is made of wire mesh covered in burlap, which gives the bees the ability to add or remove propolis (what I like to call "bee glue") to regulate the airflow.

Like most roofs, the Warre's is sloped and ventilated. It fits over the quilt box and is sturdy and heavy enough that it won't blow away. There is one downside to using a sloped roof versus the traditional Langstroth telescoping outer cover, which is what I used until the fall when I was preparing my hives for the winter. When you are inspecting your hive, you can easily set your equipment on top of a flat cover. The same can't be said for a sloped roof. Instead, you can use a spacer or what may be called an eke (basically a very shallow super) to hold your equipment.

Note: I was inspired to set up my hives in this manner by Dustin Bajer of beecentrichive.com in Edmonton, Alberta. I actually wanted to buy one of his hives, but at the time, he didn't ship.

Two Entrances

I started off my beekeeping year with one entrance, but once I had another box stacked onto my beehive, I added a second upper entrance. You can make a top entrance by making a notch in your inner cover rim or drilling a ¾-inch hole into one of your top boxes. I placed a spacer/eke, with a small opening carved out, underneath my quilt box.

A second entrance is especially important during the winter when dead bees could block the exit and kill your colony, which, on warmer days, needs to leave the hive so the bees can do their business. Another opening also improves hive ventilation, allowing excess moisture to escape.

And these are the basic pieces I used to put together a home for my bees. Now it's time for you to decide how you will set up your apiary and get your hives buzzing with bees.

project 9

how to light a smoker

Sounds easy enough, right? Until your smoker fizzles out mid-hive inspection just when you really need it. And that's why you're going to promise me you'll practice lighting your smoker — and keeping it lit — before your little bee friends arrive.

I learned this skill from a local beekeeping group for women called "The Real Queen Bees." They not only showed me how to use a smoker, they brought me out to one of their apiaries so I could see their setup in action. They spent an entire afternoon with me recounting the hard lessons they learned, which turned out to be invaluable. If you can find a similar group, I would highly encourage you to join.

The truth is you can read books, watch videos, take courses, but the most helpful of all when it comes to learning new skills is simply talking to someone who has been there and done that and crushed it. We saved ourselves thousands of dollars in mistakes by talking to other farmers and finding mentors. No one knows everything so don't be afraid to ask for help. It just might save you from being stung by your own bees.

Should you use a smoker?

I remember George telling me during my first inspection (without a smoker) that he rarely uses one unless the bees are rowdy. I had no idea what he meant by a rowdy bee until one day I opened the hive and several bees made a mad dash for my face. Yup, those were definitely rowdy bees. I quickly closed the hive and hurried to find my smoker.

Lesson #1: Even if you have gentle, well-behaved bees like mine, consider having one ready every time you open a hive so you don't have to scramble to get one lit.

Like George, I rarely use a smoker because my bees are cooperative during hive inspections. But when you need the bees to get out of the way, ignore what you are doing, or calm down when they are having a bad day (yup, bees have those too), smokers are an awesome beekeeping tool.

What does the smoke do?

A couple puffs of smoke at the hive entrance disguises any pheromones the guard bees will release to alert the hive of an impending attack.

I also learned the hard way that bees will release this same pheromone when you accidentally squish one. Bees really don't like when you kill one of their own. Within minutes, the whole cranky colony could be after you. A couple whiffs of smoke and you've prevented disaster for you, and the potentially hundreds of bees who will sting your suit and die. (You're wearing one, right?)

Light a Smoker 51

how to light a smoker

1. Wood shavings are my burning fuel of choice because that's what I always have on hand. I use small bits of wood shavings as bedding for my chickens and ducks, and this also works well in my smoker. Other beekeepers also swear by dried pine needles, pine cones, leaves, hay, or dry grass.

2. To begin, loosely crumple a piece of newspaper. Light it and use your hive tool (a metal tool that helps you pry the sticky hive boxes apart and separate your frames during inspections) to push it to the bottom of your smoker.

3. Add a handful of fuel to the fire and start pumping the bellows to keep the flame going.

4. Keep adding fuel to the fire, a little at a time, while occasionally pumping the bellows.

5. Once you have a nice fire going, continue to fill your smoker three-quarters of the way to the top with fuel. Use your hive tool to pack the fuel tightly (but not so tightly you snuff out the fire) so your smoker does what it is designed to do — smoke and not burn your bees. If you want to keep your smoker lit longer, George also recommends adding a dozen compressed wood pellets, which will smolder for many hours. Remember to keep pumping the bellows while packing to ensure your smoker doesn't burn out.

6. Close the lid and pump the bellows for a few minutes to ensure it is smoking — you do not want to see any flames coming out of the spout. The smoke should also be cool to the touch.

Your smoker will likely remain lit longer than the duration of your inspection. After I'm done, I empty any leftover contents onto our driveway and douse it with water.

WARNING

Do not use too much smoke. You'll upset your bees and taint your honey. A couple of puffs at the entrance of your hive is all that is needed, and a couple more puffs when you open the hive or when you take off a super and move down to the next. I also like to use the smoker when I'm putting the hive back together. The smoke will cause the bees to retreat down into the box so there won't be any bees hanging along the edges where they can get squished.

project 10
'success'ion planting

I may not have grown six months worth of vegetables as I said I would in my challenge, but I still had my best garden to date thanks in large part to (drum roll please) "SUCCESS"ion planting. I was up late researching when I discovered the secret to planting for success. I didn't shriek Eureka and run around the house naked, but if it wasn't so cold, I might have.

planting for plenty

Since you've already planned your garden, ordered those seeds and started some veggies indoors (you've done this, right?), you should now create a planting schedule. Doesn't that sound like fun? No? OK, well let's call it a maximizing productivity list. You're falling asleep? OK, I got it. This is a plan for Super Earth Gardeners who want to grow two or three times as many vegetables out of their same sized garden. Cool, right?

First, organize your vegetables by season so, for example, in the early spring I plant all kinds of cold hardy veggies like radishes, beets, carrots, onions, peas, turnips, potatoes, leaf lettuce, kale, and spinach. A couple weeks later I set out my cabbage, broccoli, and Brussels sprouts transplants.

As the spring temperatures rise, I sow beans and set out my squash, cucumber, tomato, and pepper transplants. And finally, after the summer solstice, I sow rutabaga. Phew! I got everything in the ground. I'm done planting, right? Nope. This all sounds good in theory, but in reality, it's not. Do you know why? Radishes will be ready to harvest in four weeks from sowing. Beets in just nine weeks. Carrots and cabbage in about 10 to 11 weeks. But your peppers and tomatoes, for example, will stay in the ground until the garden dies in the fall.

Do you see what I mean now? There are going to be big gaping holes in your garden if you don't plan in advance to fill them. You can't just plant everything and walk away. That's just for beginners who don't know what they're doing. Certainly not you and I. Oh no! We're going to plant throughout the growing season so we can get more food than we ever thought possible.

hacking your garden

Space your plantings

If you plant all your beets on the same day, they will all be ready to eat on the same day. By spacing your plantings, you'll avoid overwhelming your family with beet smoothies for breakfast, beet salads for lunch, and roasted beets for supper. Do you hear experience talking here?

Space your plantings every few weeks so fresh veggies will be available throughout the season. This is the solution to filling in those holes in your

garden. When your peas die back, for example, use the empty area to grow a second harvest of carrots. If you have the space, you can make this simpler by growing early, mid, and late maturing varieties of seeds.

Take peas, for example. Instead of remembering to plant a new crop every two weeks, you can prolong your harvest by planting early, mid, and late maturing varieties all at once. They will each be ready to devour at different times during the season so you won't ever have to fistfight with your toddler over who is going to get the last of the fresh peas.

Plan for multiple harvests

I planted my cabbage transplants into the garden in April. In May, I made a second sowing indoors so when my first cabbages were ready to pick, I had new ones to set out in the garden. I just DOUBLED my cabbage harvest. High five, Super Earth Gardener! This would work well with broccoli and cauliflower too.

Get sneaky

Interplanting is simply sowing one crop alongside another. I plant my radish and carrot seeds together in the same bed. The radishes are ready to harvest in mere weeks — way before the carrots require the additional space. Or you could plant several sowings of leaf lettuce between your tomatoes. Or you could grow kohlrabi between your cabbage and broccoli. The combinations are endless. You can go wild with this — just don't go crazy.

I don't want you to drive yourself insane trying to maximize every space in your garden, but even planning to implement one or two successions can significantly increase your harvest and transform you into the Super Earth Gardener I know you want to be. I could even have T-shirts made and we could be like Superman only we'd rescue gardens instead. Brilliant, right?

project 11
controlling pests with crop rotation

Admit it. You were thinking of skipping over this skill. Crop rotation. BORING! I hear ya. I yawned over it too until I realized I may have been ignoring one of the reasons I had to use my vacuum so often in the garden.

If you hadn't noticed by now, I'm a lazy gardener. So if a little planning in advance could save me a lot of bug vacuuming and heartache later on, I was on board.

So this year I decided to give crop rotation a try. It's actually not as overwhelming as I initially thought. Instead of planting all my veggies in the exact same bed year after year, I simply had to move them around - and remember where I planted them the next year. That may be the trickiest part. You're going to have to write this down in your garden plan.

Here's how it works.

Over time, if you keep planting your potatoes, for example, in the same location those spuds will keep eating their favourite nutrients from the soil — eventually depleting it. So what happens to your potatoes? They start producing less and just like any other living organism that doesn't eat properly, they get sick and become more susceptible to disease. Unfortunately, that's not all. Pests that love to chow down on potatoes will overwinter near or build up in the soil the longer the spuds stay in the same spot. Who wants to eat sick potatoes? Not me. So here's how to ensure your veggies stay healthy.

There are, of course, many crop rotation guides. Some of them are even divided into eight or more groups. Whoa! Way too many for me to keep track of when I can barely remember where I put my trowel two seconds ago. So I simply divided my veggies into four groups as illustrated below. It would have been easier if I could have done this randomly, but each group should be a family of vegetables, which means they are most likely all susceptible to the same diseases. For example, brassicas are all prone to clubroot, a nasty fungus affecting their roots.

peas and beans (legumes)	brassicas (broccoli, cabbage, cauliflower, Brussels sprouts, kohlrabi) and leaf crops
tomato, peppers, cucumbers, and squash (fruiting crops)	carrots, beets, and onion families (root crops)

Each year, you simply move your veggies over to a new bed. So, for example, if you plant your peas in Bed #1 this year, next year you'd move them to Bed #2. Your brassicas would then move over to Bed #3 and so on. Although your crop rotation plan probably won't be perfect — mine certainly wasn't as I moved plants around and changed my mind about how many carrots I really wanted to grow — this is a concept to keep in your gardening toolbox. So if you've planted your potatoes in the same spot for four years in a row, it's likely time for a change. But be careful. Just like succession planting, if you make your gardening plan too complicated, you will get discouraged. And cry. And curse. And wish you never made your garden so big in the first place .... You get the picture. The most important lesson I learned from crop rotation is simply to apply lots of compost to the garden so my soil doesn't become depleted and remember to keep my veggies moving — as often as I can manage.

APRIL

We considered moving into a tree house. Yes, my friend, the house renovations had finally gotten the best of us.

Many surprises were forcefully thrown at us during our first year of homesteading — escaped bees, early frosts, and broken beaks, to name a few — but none were as unexpected (and frightening) as finding lead paint in our kitchen.

Removing, repairing, or just disturbing this paint could expose our entire family to lead poisoning. Even small amounts of lead dust is dangerous, according to The World Health Organization, which also states there is no known safe level of lead exposure. We had no choice. The entire kitchen would have to be sealed off and carefully moved out. But how? My husband and I both came up with a plan.

Jérémie's plan

My husband pulled an emergency all-nighter to design a tree house that he could build and we could live in while the kitchen was being fixed. Because of how our house is laid out, he enthusiastically pointed out the next morning that I didn't have anything to worry about. We could still use the indoor bathroom without entering the kitchen area. He eagerly added that he didn't think the tree house would take too long to build since essentially it would be one room. With embarrassing visions of our neighbours (many of whom already consider us as the crazy hippies) watching in disbelief as we moved all our mattresses into our backyard tree house, I came up with my own idea.

My plan

The kids and I would move to my parents for a few weeks until the renovations were done. Needless to say, I won and the kids and I packed up our essentials and moved while Jérémie stayed behind to take care of removing all the lead paint surfaces. Although my plan was much simpler, I can't say my husband was thrilled about my idea. Truth be told, building a tree house sounded like a lot more fun than taking care of the lead paint disaster.

Now, you're probably wondering ... what did this mean for our challenge? We gave up. No, don't be silly. I convinced (begged and pleaded) my parents to allow me to raise ducks in their basement. Many farmers in our area sell chicken eggs so I thought I'd try something different. No matter that I had never even tasted a duck egg before. I had read how ducks would eat the slugs in my garden and their eggs would make my cakes rise like a dream.

So I somehow managed to convince my wonderful parents to go along with my half-baked plan. Basically, they had no idea what they were agreeing to and neither did I. Let's just say if my mom (who must have the cleanest house in all of Moncton) realized the ducks would be taking daily baths in her tub, she wouldn't have been on board.

And if I would have known that sleeping next to six ducks for three weeks would entail me waking up several times in the night to their peeping, I might have reconsidered my plan too. Ducklings may be tiny, but they can be surprisingly loud and messy.

Ducklings take particular joy in shaking their poop as far and as wide as possible. Yup, it's true. They like to shake their tail feathers. So instead of sleeping next to them, you might want to house your ducklings in a separate area such as your garage. Of course, their cuteness made up for all of these minor hardships. I mean, come on. Who can resist these faces?

In addition to the ducks, I took a course on making bar soap, discovered the "Back to Eden" gardening technique, and by the end of the month I was back at home in time to work in the garden and surprise Jérémie (who had no idea what mischief I had been up to at my parents' house) with my new feathered friends.

Raising Ducks for Eggs

Building a Duck House

Go Back to Eden

Beginner Bar Soap

project 12

raising ducks for eggs

Some people dream of owning fancy cars or taking exotic vacations. I dream of raising ducks. (Yeah, I know. You're shocked.) So when my husband recently arrived home to find six ducks and a duck house in our yard, he didn't even look surprised. I think he has simply resigned himself to the fact that his wife is determined to make his life as fun (read, difficult) as possible.

why raise ducks?

They eat slugs ... and other bugs

Throughout the summer my ducks' beaks are always covered in slimy, slug juice. They just can't seem to get enough of that mushy goodness. If you have a garden, you know how helpful a few slug-eating machines can be. I've also witnessed my ducks chowing down on worms, flies and, after a few attempts, even June bugs. Needless to say they forage for a large part of their food saving you money on feed.

> *"You don't have a slug problem; you have a duck deficiency."*
> *— Bill Mollison*

The very finest eggs

Duck eggs are the newest, coolest, foodie fashion. Compared to those of chickens, duck eggs are slightly bigger, more nutritious, and last longer in the fridge thanks to their thicker shells. If you want the fluffiest cakes and the world's best crème brûlée, you need duck eggs. They even make my gluten-free baking taste better. Simply substitute one duck egg per chicken egg in your recipe. You'll be amazed at the difference.

So what do they taste like? A lot like chicken eggs only richer thanks to their higher fat content. Personally, I think they taste better, but that could be because of how hard I worked to get them. More on that later.

They are tough

Ducks are hardier and more disease resistant than chickens. For example, while our chickens won't even put one toe in the snow, the ducks are happy to waddle around and even take a nap in it.

And unlike the chickens who hide under the eaves at the first drop of water, the ducks love the rain. One of my favourite pastimes is watching them joyfully splash and dunk their heads in one puddle after another as if they've never been in one before. They also get excited when I bring out the hose. Good luck watering your pots of flowers or vegetables. The ducks will demand their turn under the cool spray.

Their eggs won't freeze

Well, they could, but ducks lay really early in the morning so it's easy to grab the eggs before they have the chance to freeze, whereas the chickens lay all day long resulting in the occasional frozen egg if I'm not careful.

You don't have to clip their wings

Domesticated ducks have been bred so they're too heavy to fly, unlike my chickens who will easily fly over garden fences in search of their favourite veggies.

They won't tear up your garden

Chickens love to scratch, but ducks won't harm your garden with their webbed feet — unless you have small seedlings. In that case, the ducks will trample them.

what you'll need

Find a source

We bought our ducks from Rick's Funny Farm in Amherst, Nova Scotia. Maybe you can find a local source too, but if not, you can buy them online. Ideally, your source would be willing to sex your birds so you don't end up with several males like we did — unless you're OK with butchering them for roasted duck.

Now if you've ever seen a duckling, you know just how irresistible they are with their big, webbed feet and fluffy, down feathers. I had planned to buy three ducklings. But when I got to Rick's Funny Farm I succumbed to their cuteness and ended up with six — four Khaki Campbells and two Saxonys, both of which are *egg*cellent egg layers.

My parents were thrilled with the extra ducks, by the way.

Whatever you do, don't buy just one. They need the companionship of fellow ducks — and no, chickens won't do.

Purchase a heat lamp

You will need to invest in a heat lamp to keep your ducks warm for the first few weeks. I use the Brooder Hen and highly recommend it. It is adjustable so you can raise its height as the ducklings grow.

Housing

I wasn't prepared for the mess my ducklings would make. They tried to swim in their water, threw their food across every surface, and shook their poop with abandon. The best solution we came up with was to line a large box with plastic and fill it with wood shavings, which I scooped out and replaced on a daily basis.

Warning: Ducklings grow fast. Start with a larger box than what you think you'll need.

Food and water

If you've previously raised chickens, you might be tempted to feed your ducks the same feed. It is not recommended, but if your local feed store doesn't carry duck starter, you can feed chick starter as long as it's not medicated and you add niacin. Waterfowl have a higher requirement for niacin than chickens. I solved this problem by adding a couple tablespoons of brewer's yeast per duck to their feed.

Our ducks were also treated to the finest dandelion leaves and clumps of grass courtesy of the kids who went on daily "duck food" hunts. If you are feeding your flock any fresh greens or other treats, you'll also need to supply them with grit. Ducks don't have teeth. Instead they use small rocks to help break up their food.

> **NOTE**
>
> Your ducks won't be happy with just a typical chicken waterer. They also need to be able to clean and rinse out their bills and nostrils. A simple solution is to cut a hole in a bucket or water jug.

To swim or not to swim?

Although I've read ducks don't *need* access to swimming water, mine love to clean themselves. I gave my ducklings regular baths in the tub. Now they have their own kiddie pool as well as a running stream (OK, it's really a ditch) where they splash around on a daily basis.

Once your ducks are around 6 to 8 weeks of age and are fully feathered, they can be moved outdoors with shelter from predators, which brings us to the next skill.

project 13
building a duck house

Nightfall. My ducks are still standing outside their coop — not in their house where they are supposed to spend the night safely tucked away from predators.

I tried everything to coax them inside. First, I bribed them with a trail of their favourite snack food (peas) from the bottom of their ramp and into their coop. And did they follow that trail? Oh no! They tried to eat the peas from the side of the ramp. One or two of the smarter ones finally got the hint, but then came out of the coop before the others even had a chance to get inside. I tried herding them and shouting at them. I tried chasing them. Nothing worked.

So every evening I would find myself running in circles around the duck house chasing after and, if I was lucky, eventually capturing each duck and putting them into their house. And no, in case you are wondering, it's not easy outsprinting a scared duck. By the end of this game, I was sweating and ready for a shower.

This was the routine for weeks — until I hatched up a desperate plan. I would duck keep like a ninja. I hid outside until it was completely dark — so dark the ducks finally decided to go into their house all by themselves. Success! Except the door was still open.

Somehow I had to close it without startling the ducks. If they heard me coming near, they would make a panicked exit. So I sprinted towards the coop as fast as I could from where I was hiding.

I likely would have made it before the ducks even knew what was happening except I forgot I left my wheelbarrow outside. Of course, I very painfully tripped over and into it. As I nursed my wounds, all I could hear were those ducks, now back outside, quack, quack, quaking away. Apparently they were having a good laugh at my expense.

Eventually I did figure out why the ducks wouldn't go inside their home — they were terrified of the ramp. Most of the cute duck houses you can find online have one. But I can confidently write that ducks do not like them — or at least my ducks don't. Their house should sit directly on the ground with a predator-proof floor such as wire mesh and wood or concrete.

Over time, they will get used to the ramp, but if you don't have the patience to chase your ducks for days on end, I would advise against it.

a few more tips for building a duck house

Size
A duck house should be sized to accommodate 4 square feet per bird. I thought this sounded like a lot of space for a couple ducks so our house is about half that size. I didn't realize domesticated fowl such as my Saxonys would grow to be bigger than the wild ducks you may occasionally see in the park or in your yard. Ducks also need plenty of room to stretch their wings.

However, our ducks only spend the night in their house. In the morning, they have free roam of our entire yard. If your ducks do not have outdoor space, they will definitely need the extra room.

Flooring
The floor of our duck house is lined with a piece of vinyl. As I mentioned earlier, ducks are messy and love to play in their drinking water. The vinyl prevents the floor of your coop from rotting over time and makes clean-up easier.

Bedding
I use wood shavings although a combination of wood shavings and straw would work better. Why? The ducks splash so much water their shavings become completely sodden and trampled. Straw, on the other hand, holds its shape and is slightly warmer.

Air flow
Our duck house is about 3½ feet tall with vents near the roof to allow for good air flow. Ventilation is crucial. If moisture can't escape, it can lead to mouldy bedding and sick ducks. Our vents are covered in ¼-inch wire mesh to prevent predators from entering.

Door
The door on our duck house is about 10 inches wide by 15 inches tall. It is recommended to make the opening a little wider so that if two ducks decide to go in at once, they won't get stuck. I only wish I would have had this problem.

Clean up
Our duck house has large double doors on the side that allow me to easily change their bedding and provide them fresh food and water.

Nesting boxes
You don't have to worry about nesting boxes as ducks will lay in a corner of their home — or at least they should. Two out of our three female ducks laid in the coop. The other one decided to make her own nest outdoors. And just to keep things fun and interesting, every time we'd locate the nest, she'd make a new one somewhere else for us to find the next day. It's like an Easter egg hunt every morning. It's so much fun! Not.

These tips are likely all you need to put together a cozy home for your flock — one that doesn't result in you having to chase your ducks in circles late into the evening as your husband watches in laughter.

project 14

going back to Eden

Sell your tiller. Put away your hose. Forget about weeding. We're going Back to Eden.

I was once again reading late at night (this time while wearing ear plugs to drown out the quacking of those dratted ducklings) when I discovered the solution to my problem: What do I do with all the spoiled bedding from my ducks?

I wish I could say I had this all planned out, but by a stroke of genius, accidental luck, I located our duck house beside the garden so as I emptied its contents every day, I could simply shovel and toss the bedding into the garden or leave it in a pile to be composted for later application.

I did use the wheel barrow for the parts of the garden that were farther away but overall this was an easy task. And most exciting of all — it worked. I piled the wood shavings in abundance with surprising results.

First, our soil didn't disappear. We live in an open, windy area that easily carries away our hard earned compost and leaves craters in our garden beds. The wood shavings were just heavy enough to hold down our precious top soil.

Second, the weeds disappeared like magic. OK, a week after covering them, more popped up through the mulch. But as time went on, they were much easier to remove.

Third, if you stuck your hand in the soil underneath the mulch, it was not dry, crusty, sun baked dust, but moist, loose soil that looked like black gold. The mulch was preventing the soil from compacting and the sun from evaporating the water.

As the garden flourished under the mulch, I basked in my moment of glory. I have to say it felt good. My garden successes have been few and far between. This was a big win.

This method of gardening is similar to "Back to Eden." The creator, Paul Gautschi, describes walking in the forest and noticing how, despite the heat and drought, the forest floor was moist. Why? It was covered in mulch. In fact, nowhere in nature do you find bare soil. If you do, panic. There is likely something wrong.

So Paul decided to apply the same concept to his garden. By covering his beds with fine wood chips (not the big pieces) mixed with leaves and needles, he improved, protected, and kept moisture in the soil. Wood chips are Paul's preferred mulch, but you can use whatever natural materials you happen to have on hand including straw or leaves.

Now, this doesn't mean you don't need to apply compost to your soil. You likely do. The mulch goes on top of the compost. You also don't mix the wood chips into your soil or you could rob the earth of nitrogen, a critical nutrient your veggies need to grow.

If this is your first garden, consider adding cardboard and/or newspapers directly on top of your lawn in the fall. Cover with compost and then mulch. By the spring, you will have eliminated or at least controlled the amount of weeds in your garden.

This is what our neighbours did to start their garden with much less effort and much better results than our own. Instead, we went to the trouble of removing the grass and then planted. I would never do this again.

Should you till first? No. Actually, you NEVER till your soil using the Back to Eden method. You let the worms, the plants' roots, and the many soil microorganisms do this work for you.

When it's time to plant your garden, you simply brush the wood chips aside, sow your seeds or transplant your seedlings into the soil, and brush back the wood chips.

So where do you find mulch if you don't have your own source? Many cities or municipalities, tree services, or electric companies will collect branches and leaves that are ground or chipped into a mulch. You might be able to claim this "waste" for free. We have also gone undercover and stolen bagged leaves that have been left for the local garbage collection.

I didn't have enough wood to start testing the Back to Eden method until later in the gardening season (and only on parts of it) as you will notice from some of the pictures of my garden. But even with just a couple months of experimenting, I hope to never garden with bare soil again.

project 15

beginner bar soap

Some people collect comic books, coins or antiques, I collect bars of soap. So when I go on vacation, I like to seek out specialty soap stores and blissfully bury my nose in one beautiful scented variety after another. And then dream of making my own from the honey and wax I harvest from my hives.

Up until recently I've been afraid of using lye, a caustic chemical that can burn your skin and even blind you. But when I saw an advertisement for a soap workshop with ZOLI Handcrafted Soaps in Memramcook, New Brunswick, I knew I had to try making my own.

It turns out lye is not as scary as I originally thought — as long as you take the proper safety precautions like stylish goggles and gloves. You'll also want to wear long sleeves. You can save your flowy, Boho clothes for another day. You'll want to wear something snug fitting.

Jeanne Hebert of ZOLI Handcrafted Soaps describes this recipe as a great beginner soap. The oils used are inexpensive (just in case it doesn't work out your first try) and it has a short tracing time (the time it takes for the soap to thicken enough for you to pour into your moulds).

I love that this recipe uses tallow. Not only is it inexpensive, but it is essentially a waste product that doesn't need as much processing as many vegetable oils, which have to be harvested, pressed, filtered, bottled, and transported, in my case, a very long distance. How much energy does that consume versus saving the fat from your beef dinner?

Now, if you don't happen to have any stored in your cupboard, you may be wondering where to buy tallow. You don't. You make your own. How do you do that? Well, I really shouldn't tell you. You see, my publishers have told me I'm only allowed 52 skills in this book and I've already broken the rules by sneaking in a 53rd. But technically, I've already tried this one before. So I'm just going to add this extra one right here in the middle of making bar soap and hope they don't notice. It will be our little secret, OK?

ingredients

- 1.28 lbs tallow
- 6.84 oz vegetable oil (any kind)
- 3.06 oz lye
- 8.88 oz distilled water
- 30 drops of essential oil of your choice

NOTE
Although you need lye to make soap, there won't be any lye in your finished product. The lye will evaporate, making it safe for you to suds up with in the tub.

supplies

- soap moulds
- parchment paper or oil for lining/greasing your moulds
- plastic wrap and blankets
- stainless steel pot
- stainless steel bowl
- wooden spoon or hand-held mixer for mixing
- thermometer
- goggles and gloves

how to render tallow

First, you'll need to call your local butcher and ask for suet (beef fat). Cut any meat from the suet, which can spoil your tallow. Place the fat into a stockpot and add enough water to cover the suet as well as 1 tablespoon of salt for every pound of fat.

Bring to a boil and simmer on low until the fat turns into melted tallow. Meanwhile, line a colander with cheesecloth and place on top of another pot.

Pour the tallow into the colander and let cool to room temperature. Store in your fridge overnight.

In the morning, there should be a large, white disc of fat on top of your pot. That's tallow! It's not only an inexpensive ingredient, but used in this recipe, it produces a long-lasting, hard bar of soap with a rich, creamy lather.

1. Line your moulds with parchment paper, or for silicone moulds, you can use oil (olive, vegetable, or coconut). Instead of using moulds, we simply lined cardboard boxes with plastic to make bars of soap.

2. Carefully weigh and measure all your ingredients.

3. Measure your water and slowly add the lye while constantly mixing. Always add small amounts of the lye to the water and not vice versa or you could create a lye explosion. You definitely do not want this to happen. Once all the lye has dissolved, you can move on to your oil mixture.

4. Heat your oil in a stainless steel pot on medium-low until the temperature reaches 140°F to 150°F. You want both your lye mixture and oils to cool to 100°F to 110°F. As you wait, continue to mix and take the temperature. Mixing will prevent clumps in your soap and bring down the temperature faster.

5. Once the oil has cooled to the proper temperature, pour the oil slowly into the lye and water mixture in a stainless steel container.

6. Just keep stirring! Use a wooden spoon or, for quicker results, a hand-held mixer until your soap becomes the consistency of pudding. This is called tracing. You can test if your soap is ready by slowly drizzling it with a spoon. If you see the line in your soap, it is ready to mould.

7. Mix in several drops of your favourite essential oils.

8. Pour the soap mixture into your lined or oiled mould and cover with plastic wrap and blankets to keep it warm. You want to bring the temperature down as slowly as possible to achieve a hard bar of soap.

9. Within 1 to 2 days, the soap will be hard enough to de-mould and cut (if you are making bar soap like we did). Always use gloves for this step since the lye is still active and not completely evaporated.

10. Let your soap cure for three weeks. Turn the bars (using gloves) every week or so to promote good air flow on all sides of the soap.

And voilà! It's only April and you've already begun your Christmas shopping. You could pair your soap with a tube of homemade lip balm (Project 33 on Page 144) and a jar of healing hand salve (Project 32 on Page 142). Not only are these gifts inexpensive, but they're thoughtful, unique, and useful presents anyone would enjoy receiving — including me in case you're wondering.

#1 NOTE Only certain materials can be used for cold process soap: plastic, silicone, and wood. Active lye will rust most metals and the heat from the lye will melt weaker plastics.

#3 NOTE Carry out this step in a well ventilated area. The fumes are toxic.

MAY

This month starts with a dehydrated package of gluten-free sourdough starter.

And then a second package. And then a third package ….

It turns out making gluten-free sourdough isn't the easiest homesteading activity. It took me months to get my sourdough active enough to make bread. In fact, I may have gone a little sourdough crazy.

It was a Friday night and I was actually debating whether Jérémie and I should risk going out for supper because I might not be home in time to feed my baby (a.k.a. gluten-free sourdough starter). You see, sourdough (especially the gluten-free kind I craved) requires that you feed it about every four hours (yes, I actually considered getting up in the night to feed it, but it turns out I like sleep more than I like bread), keep it at the perfect temperature, and carefully monitor its activity.

What I really needed was a sourdough babysitter — which apparently actually exists, but only in Stockholm according to my investigations. Apparently, the Swedes share my dilemma.

Instead of forgoing vacation (because what would happen to your precious sourdough?), I read that the Swedes can leave it at the airport with a sitter. Problem solved! But I'm pretty sure if I had suggested hiring a sourdough sitter to my husband, he would have thrown this particular "baby" out the window.

So off we went to dinner. I still had no idea how obsessed I was until I came home that evening and instead of immediately asking how the kids were, my first question was, "How's the sourdough?"

I have to admit my first experiments were more like eating toasted bricks with a chewy centre. Jérémie would only eat my bread toasted with cheese. On my blog I announced I had made the world's 259th best gluten-free sourdough bread that, if I'm being honest, was an optimistic statement. (You'll be happy to hear my sourdough bread-making skills have advanced since that original post and the recipe I share here is a much improved, definitely not brick-like, version.)

When I wasn't obsessing over sourdough, I was crying over dead fruit trees. Alas, the sourdough wasn't our only failure this month. We lost almost half of our fruit trees to voles that feasted on their roots and bark. We found multiple tree victims lying wasted on the ground with roots chewed to bits.

After spending hours planting the trees and hundreds of dollars purchasing them, I was disheartened to say the least. I had envisioned the front of our property as an orchard filled with specialty fruit and nut trees. Instead, I was creating a tree cemetery.

Thankfully, we were able to save the remaining fruit trees by surrounding them with rock and covering the trunks in wire mesh from top to bottom. After some late night research, I discovered that voles do not like open ground. So we also made plans to invest in several Olde English Babydoll Southdown Sheep, a rare breed with teddy bear faces and wool as soft as cashmere.

Since Babydoll Sheep are naturally shorter than typical breeds (24 inches tall at the shoulder) and therefore can't reach very high, they're often used in orchards and vineyards to mow and fertilize between the trees and vines.

Not only are sheep a more environmentally friendly choice, I won't have to spend my time hauling fertilizer or pushing a lawnmower. In case you're wondering … yes, we'd rather feed and care for animals every single day of the year than mow our lawn.

Unfortunately, we were so busy vole proofing our trees and making sourdough we didn't notice the wood we had collected to make our compost bins was slowly being stolen — by our kids. Instead of a compost bin, they spent the month building a fort. Ahhhh … the joys of homesteading with kids.

Full disclosure: Planting fruit trees and raspberry canes (two of the skills this month) are activities we had tried prior to moving to the farm and thought we had succeeded at — until we discovered the sad truth one year later. So both activities went back on our list of skills to learn correctly. I hope we finally planted them properly — time will tell!

Gluten-Free Sourdough Bread

How NOT to Plant a Raspberry Cane

How NOT to Grow a Fruit Tree

Learn to Compost

project 16

gluten-free sourdough bread

I had watched my grandmother make bread. My aunt made bread. My neighbours make bread. I believed it was easy. Ha, I thought, I'm going to nail this skill in no time.

As you know from reading the introduction to this chapter, that's not how things unfolded. Making sourdough bread is tricky. Making gluten-free sourdough bread that actually tastes good is downright challenging. So what's the secret formula? Stubbornness. You don't give up. You keep trying until you create bread so good it was worth the several packages of starter and multiple bags of flour in which you had to invest to make it. Now, you may be wondering why I wanted to make sourdough versus traditional bread. Yes, there is a reason other than making things difficult for myself. It's healthier. Here's why:

what is sourdough?

Until a few centuries ago, we all ate sourdough. Commercial baker's yeast was not available to our ancestors. Instead, they fermented flour and water. The combination of wild yeast from the air and the lactic acid bacteria found in flour is what makes the bread rise and gives it its superpower.

As a fermented food, sourdough is easier to digest, more nutritious than regular bread, and will increase your lifespan by several years. OK, I don't know if this last comment is true, but it could be. So go ahead and order that sourdough starter. I purchased mine from Cultures for Health.

activating your sourdough starter

These are the instructions for activating your starter, which I followed exactly the second time after my first one failed.

ingredients

- 3 tbsp ground chia seeds
- ½ cup rice flour, plus more for dusting
- ⅓ cup sorghum flour
- ¼ cup millet flour
- ½ cup warm water
- 1½ tsp salt
- ⅓ cup tapioca flour
- 2½ tsp blackstrap molasses
- 1 whole egg
- 2 egg whites
- 1 tbsp olive oil
- 2 cups sourdough starter

supplies

- 1 packet dehydrated sourdough starter
- brown rice flour
- chlorine and fluoride free water
- quart-size mason jar
- cheesecloth
- non-aluminium mixing utensil

instructions

1. Mix your sourdough starter together with 1 tbsp of brown rice flour and 1 tbsp of room temperature water in a quart-size mason jar. Stir thoroughly. Cover the jar with cheesecloth or another breathable material and secure with the band of your mason jar. Leave the starter in a warm place for 4 to 8 hours. I keep mine in the oven with the light on.

2. After 4 to 8 hours, feed the starter an additional 2 tbsp of flour and 2 tbsp of water. Mix thoroughly. Now take a look at the starter. Does it seem to have the consistency of pancake batter? If not, you may need to add a little more flour or water.

3. After 4 to 8 hours, feed the starter an additional ¼ cup of flour and ¼ cup of water. Stir vigorously and add more flour or water if necessary.

4. After another 4 to 8 hours, feed the starter with an additional ¼ cup of flour and ¼ cup of water. Mix well and add more flour or water if necessary.

5. Discard (but don't throw away) all but ½ cup of your starter. Save the discarded starter and use it in your morning pancakes.

6. Then feed the remaining starter with ½ cup of water and ½ cup flour. Repeat every 4 to 8 hours for 3 to 7 days until the starter has the consistency of pancake batter and is bubbling regularly within a few hours of feeding.

Are you ready to bake bread?

NO

Store your sourdough starter in the fridge. It will go into hibernation and you will only have to feed it every three to four days.

NOTE
Once you are ready to make bread, you will have to allow your starter to warm to room temperature and then feed it two or three times according to the following instructions before using it to bake bread.

YES

Continue to feed your starter once every 4 to 8 hours using 1 part starter, 1 part water, and 1 part flour. I discarded all but a ½ cup of my starter at each feeding until I was ready to bake my bread. At this point, I stopped discarding and kept feeding the starter according to the 1 part starter, 1 part water, and 1 part flour ratio until I had built up enough starter for my recipe. Your sourdough starter will be ready to use in your bread recipe within 2 hours after the last feeding. Don't forget to reserve at least ¼ cup of your starter so you can continue making bread.

steps

1. Blend the chia seeds with ½ cup rice, sorghum, and millet flours. Use a non-aluminium mixing utensil for all the steps.

2. In a separate bowl, mix together the water, salt, tapioca flour, and molasses.

3. Add the egg, egg whites, and olive oil to the molasses mixture and stir well.

4. Mix your sourdough starter and your dry ingredients together and add to your wet ingredients. Blend well. Your mixture should be more wet than doughy. Add about 1½ tbsp of rice flour if needed.

5. Butter your bread pan and dust millet flour all over the bottom and sides. Pour your sourdough mixture into the pan and let rise for 4 to 8 hours or until the bread nearly doubles in size. Cover in aluminium foil.

6. Set a metal pan on your oven floor and preheat your oven to 425°F. When the temperature reaches approximately 375°F, carefully place your bread inside and a cup of hot tap water in the pan. This helps form a crispy, brown crust. Bake for 45 minutes. Remove the aluminium foil after 20 minutes of cooking.

lessons learned

Feed that sourdough
One of the reasons it took so long for my starter to activate was because I wasn't feeding it often enough. During the day, I now feed my sourdough 1 part starter, 1 part water, and 1 part flour every four to six hours.

Sourdough likes it hot, but not too hot
Sourdough likes to be kept at a much warmer temperature than our room temperature of 17°C. Instead, it prefers temperatures between 21°C and 30°C. I keep our sourdough in the oven with the light turned on.

Bubbling success
Once your starter is bubbling (you should actually see the bubbles surface and pop) and doubling in size between feedings, it's time to make bread. And voilà! Now slice yourself a little piece of sourdough heaven. Or toast it with cheese. I won't judge.

project 17
how NOT to plant a raspberry cane

I planted a stick.

OK, it's technically called a bare root raspberry "cane," but I'm telling you it looked like yours truly paid $8.99 for a stick. The tag, however, informed me it was indeed going to produce pints of lush, red, melt-in-your-mouth berries.

So I simply dug a hole and the kids and I stuck that thing in the ground. I walked away as smug as could be thinking, 'that was easy.' Later, I consulted my friend Google. This is farming lesson No. 1. Always do your research before you plant.

It is advised to soak your stick for a couple hours before planting and to spread a couple inches of compost to the TOP of the soil after planting to add nutrients to the soil and hopefully improve your raspberry yield. The base of the raspberry should also be mulched to insulate the roots during winter and keep weeds at bay. Raspberries have shallow roots so weeding must be done carefully. Better to put down mulch.

Now the directions on the tag said you should plant red raspberries three feet apart in rows eight feet apart. I scoffed a little at this, thinking my stick doesn't need that much room.

WARNING! WARNING! WARNING! Red raspberries do indeed spread — A LOT.

Red raspberries spread away from the original planting site by sending up new canes called 'suckers' away from the original root crown. So don't … ahem … put a red raspberry bush say, for a random example, as a border in the middle of your planned vegetable garden area. But who would be stupid enough to do that anyway?

So this was my original stick...

And this is my raspberry bush one year later.

In one year! I was amazed. Maybe you are too, but knowledgeable farmers are now rolling their eyes and laughing because I didn't realize raspberries need to be pruned. Summer raspberries are pruned after fruiting by cutting out the old canes and leaving the new to grow. Fall fruiting varieties are cut to the ground in early winter or as soon as they are done fruiting.

Pruning only takes a few minutes and increases your yield, but I didn't do it. Hence the "wild" look of my bush. You may also notice they are planted in front of a fence. How the heck did I think I was going to harvest the berries on the other side?

Thankfully raspberries are very forgiving and despite all these errors I was able to harvest a few pints of fresh raspberries. In fact, I'm told these are the easiest fruit to grow. So if you have any unused plot of ground maybe covered in grass that you hate mowing, a raspberry cane is your answer. They don't need the best soil (they will grow in most kinds), you don't even need full sun (raspberries do just fine in partial shade although you may get a little less fruit), and a year later you'll be harvesting delicious red gems that you can then use to make pie.

Unfortunately, I didn't. A little raspberry goblin gobbled all the raspberries off my bush before they could even make it into the house.

Oh, you thought I meant one of the kids? No, it was me. Sadly, I had to buy raspberries. But next year, after pruning my bush, I'll be making jam and pie with homegrown berries and hopefully you will too.

project 18

how NOT to grow a fruit tree

I come up with the most creative ways to fail.

Take this peach tree, for example. I accidentally planted it in an ant's nest. Who fails to notice ants crawling everywhere in the hole they're digging? I'm pretty sure the answer is — only me!

Planting fruit trees is a skill I had been dreaming about since I took Geoff Lawton's Permaculture Design Course. In Geoff's words, permaculture is "a system of design that provides all of the needs for humanity in a way that benefits the environment."

During the program, I fell in love with the idea of growing a food forest where I could leisurely walk and pluck my breakfast from its branches.

When we arrived at our almost completely deforested homestead, I couldn't wait to begin. As I was taught in permaculture, I wanted to map out the contours (a level area across a slope) of our farm.

By planting on contour and digging swales (basically ditches designed to hold and evenly distribute water instead of draining it away) along them, you can not only increase the diversity of life on your land, but slow the flow of rain water, raise your ground water levels, prevent erosion, and ensure your trees never go thirsty again. You can even reverse desertification using swales. Basically, a swale is an amazing permaculture tool and I couldn't wait to see its land rejuvenating benefits in action.

So we bought a transit level, which allowed us to easily locate and then stake out the contours of our land. Unfortunately, when we called a local company to price out digging the two-foot deep swales across our 12 acres of land, the cost was thousands of dollars we didn't have.

I was discouraged. We may end up having to dig our swales by hand. Nevertheless I thought we might as well plant a few fruit trees. So that's what we did — even before we embarked on our challenge. So why is this skill part of our quest? I wanted to finally learn how to do this properly because our first tries were mediocre to say the least. And that's OK.

If you (like us!) have failed miserably many times before, you can celebrate. Your chances of success have drastically increased. The bigger your failure, the more opportunities you have to learn. Yeah, I know how painful it is to mess up, but I'm pretty sure all homesteaders make mistakes. So instead of seeing your misadventures as failures, look at these lessons as great catalysts towards your success.

Here are a few of the best lessons we've learned along the way.

Don't plant your fruit tree in an ant's nest
Enough said.

Be wary of the half-price-off trees at the end of the season
I know, they look like great deals. They probably already have small fruit on them. But be careful. They will need extra care in order to get their roots established before winter. It can be done, but personally, I had more luck with bare root trees that I planted in the spring than the half-price potted trees I planted in the middle of summer.

Find your zone
When deciding which fruit trees to grow on your property ensure you choose one that will fruit in your zone. For example, we planted two Northern Pecans, which grow well in our area but, as I recently discovered, they may never set fruit. Of course, I'm not disappointed because as I pointed out earlier this is just another learning experience. Sniff. Sniff.

Check pollination requirements
We have a 5-year-old Foffonof plum tree on our property that doesn't set fruit. I now know why. It doesn't have a pollinator. This tree should be pollinated by the Canadian plum (*Prunus nigra*). Some trees are self-fertile, which means they don't require another tree for pollination. Other trees like the Foffonof need another variety in order to set fruit.

Beware. Rodents can kill.

I didn't even know what a vole was until they ate the roots of my fruit trees and I found the chewed victims lying on the ground. To deter voles and other rodents ensure your trees are wrapped with guards and surround your trees' trunks in ¼-inch wire mesh. If you can, bury it a couple of inches into the ground. Finally, keep a large area of cleared space around your trees as voles tend to avoid open areas. And then, pray for predators.

Dig a proper hole

You may have a tree that doesn't seem to thrive or dies for what seems like no apparent reason. You may scratch your head and hum and haw and then finally decide to pull it out of the ground only to discover it was root bound. Its roots didn't find their way into the surrounding area.

Help your tree reach into the surrounding earth by spreading its roots and creating grooves in the sides and bottom of your hole.

Get yourself some all-star plants and trees

I'm talking about companion plants. I may have found them too confusing to use in my annual garden, but I have heard from urban growers such as Codiac Organics in Moncton, New Brunswick, that this system works well with perennials. Here are few examples of these "nurse" plants:

Yarrow produces nectar sought by predatory insects that feed on fruit tree pests.

Hyssop confuses pests with its aromatic scent.

Bocking 4 Comfrey suppresses weeds and draws minerals and nutrients from deep within the soil. Chop and drop its leaves throughout the growing season for a nutritious mulch for your trees.

However, since we are switching to a grazing system around our trees, I don't know if this would work as well on a large scale with only two people to manage what I hope will be hundreds of trees someday. However, all is not lost.

I planted companion "nitrogen-fixing" trees instead, following the example of Miracle Farms, a permaculture orchard in Quebec.

What is a nitrogen-fixing tree? Through a partnership with microorganisms in their roots, these trees can turn atmospheric nitrogen into fertilizer, which can be used by the tree itself as well as other trees and plants in its immediate area through root die back, leaf fall, and chop and drop pruning.

As is done at Miracle Farms, I planted one nitrogen fixing tree (Black Locust) followed by two fruit or nut trees. Black Locust is a fast-growing, drought-resistant tree with extremely fragrant white flowers beloved by the bees. Its hard, rot-resistant lumber is prized for burning and fence posts. These are all great qualities, but I chose it because it was the cheapest. I later learned they were cheap for a reason. Their branches are covered with two-inch thorns.

These are the kind of trees you might plant around the perimeter of your property to discourage trespassers. I planted them as lovely additions to my orchard. You may want to consider a thornless Honeylocust (as is used at Miracle Farms) or another nitrogen-fixing tree instead.

If you have the space to plant several fruit trees, try mixing them up. For example, at Miracle Farms, they plant one apple, one pear or plum followed by a nitrogen-fixing tree. This cuts down on pests in the orchard who can't easily find their way from one apple tree, for example, to the next.

Feed your tree

Cardboard, compost, mulch … Repeat after me … cardboard, compost, mulch. Young trees have a hard time competing with grass for nutrients so your best bet is to place corrugated cardboard around your tree (but not directly at the base) and top with compost and mulch.

Now all you have to do is wait. And wait. And wait. And in two to seven years, you will finally get to sink your teeth into that fresh, crispy apple, that ripe, juicy pear, or that sweet, sun-ripened cherry. Totally worth the wait, right? What? You find seven years a long time? Well, think of it this way. How much easier would it be if we could grow carrots on trees, for example? You would only have to plant them once and they would come back year after year after year. Fruit trees will continue to provide your homestead with succulent, fresh fruit for decades to come. Now that's a sweet gift worth waiting for!

project 19

learn to compost

Mary, Mary, quite contrary. How does your garden grow?

Compost.

Compost is the best fertilizer for your vegetables. Period.

We spent $300 worth in compost to get our first garden started, and I still can't believe we spent that much for what was essentially old cow poop.

Never again.

So we started composting simply by saving our kitchen waste in an old stainless steel pot. That was easy — until it got full. Now what?

Well, my husband said he'd build a compost bin. As I waited impatiently for this to happen, my pot overflowed. So what did I do? I followed my grandma's very practical methods: I found an inconspicuous spot in the backyard and dumped it or simply buried bits and pieces in the ground. Hey, whatever works, right?

Before we added chickens and ducks to the farm, the only materials we really had to compost were kitchen scraps and, for at least part of the year, weeds and leaves. So I would add these to the pile when I could and turned and watered it when I remembered. (The microbes that live in your compost pile are demanding fellows who need a bit of air to breathe and moisture to drink.)

Halfway through the summer, we were gifted an old plastic recycling bin. I put this in the garden and started filling it with scraps, weeds, and leaves too. In the end, I think Grandma's pile method is simpler because when I wanted to turn the compost, I didn't have to shovel it out first.

The end. That's it? Yup, composting just happens — even if you don't turn your pile or water it. But I have to admit that it didn't happen as quickly as it could have if I would have had the correct size (at least 3 feet tall by 3 feet wide) and the correct ratio of carbon to nitrogen ratio (about 30:1). For example, the carbon to nitrogen ratio of chicken manure is about 10:1.

If the C:N ratio is too high (excess carbon), decomposition slows. If the C:N ratio is too low (excess nitrogen), your pile will stink.

So the composting method we were using wasn't ideal, but it was the best we could do with the materials we had until we got chickens. That's when everything changed.

All those leftover food scraps were now given to them. I simply brought my pot of kitchen scraps out to the coop and dumped it on top of their wood shavings. The chickens would excitedly scratch and turn everything including their own manure and urine — essentially doing the job of aerating the compost. Those chickens were making compost better than I could!

Every day I would add more scraps and every few days to a week, I would simply add more wood shavings. The chickens would

devour the treats I provided as well as any bugs they could find in the compost — a little extra free food for your flock.

So how is our coop set up? We have a dirt floor with wire mesh buried underneath to prevent rodents from burrowing inside. On top of the dirt we spread wood shavings. Next year, we also hope to use the leaves our neighbours are eager to get rid of in the fall.

The door of the coop is about a foot and half off the ground to accommodate all the extra bedding. At this height we never have to worry about not being able to open the door.

Another name for this method of composting is deep litter. Basically, chicken manure, which is high in nitrogen, and wood chips, a source of carbon, accumulate and decompose inside the coop all winter.

In the spring, you can congratulate yourself. You just won the compost lottery. And you were excited about the eggs the chickens were going to give you. Pshhh ... FREE COMPOST, BABY! That's why you want chickens.

JUNE

Homesteading books often paint rosy, romantic pictures about what life is like on the farm. You may longingly look at eye-catching, manicured gardens, smile at cute, well-behaved farm animals (standing inside their fence where they are supposed to be), and happily imagine your own kids joyfully helping in the garden with big smiles on their faces.

Well, this month I learned what the reality actually is. Let's just say it's not so picture perfect. Real farm life is:

Scary

How would you feel about driving your car with thousands of live bees buzzing in your back seat? Yeah, that's how I felt too. This month I collected my honeybee colony and settled them in their new home. I wasn't nervous until I watched as George (my beekeeping mentor as you may recall) blocked the hive entrances with a small piece of toilet paper. He then loaded my two hives in the back seat of my car.

That's it? I thought. Toilet paper is the only thing stopping thousands of bees from flying around my car? Shouldn't he be taking some other protective measures? Nope. I was assured I was going to be just fine. Let's just say I have never driven so carefully in my entire life. Thankfully, we arrived home without incident; I set the hives on their stands, removed the toilet paper from their entrances, and ran towards the house like the whole colony was chasing after me. In reality, the bees couldn't be bothered. But I wasn't taking any chances.

Messy

This was also the month we brought home our 1-day-old chicks. It was still too cool to keep them outside so I made a home for them in a box in my dining room. Why the dining room? I thought it would be fun to watch them as we ate our meals. It would be like having our own dinner theatre. And it was entertaining — at first.

Chicks (surprise!) kick up a lot of dust, which settles in thick layers over everything — including your kitchen table. A little chicken dust in your potatoes, anyone?

Frustrating

I tell the kids at least three times a day to remember to close the gate after foraging in the garden. Yet it was me who forgot.

Curious why they weren't normally allowed in the garden, all the ducks waddled their way into my vegetable patch where they excitedly nibbled and trampled all my cucumber, bean, and pea seedlings. Tired from all this munching and waddling around, they decided to have a cozy nap on top of my carrots. Until, of course, I rudely woke them with my screaming.

Challenging

And then there are my kids. Are we smiling and laughing as we plant and tend the garden? Are you kidding me? Ella, who is now old enough to actually help, gets bored at the tedious tasks rather quickly and "needs" to go play on the swings.

On the other hand, Jack loves to help. He takes the hose and gets nice and close to the plants and then waters them at full blast. He "weeds" my garden of all the good stuff and harvests most vegetables by pulling up the entire plant. And he can never quite figure out where the beds are and where the path is because I always seem to find him standing on the vegetables.

Magical

If homesteading is so scary, messy, frustrating, and challenging, you may wonder why I don't give up.

It's true. Farm life hasn't turned out to be as enchanting and definitely not as easy as I had hoped, but nothing I've ever done has been as rewarding, as satisfying, or as meaningful. The magic is in the simple moments like these:

- Waking up early and sneaking outside with my morning cup of tea to enjoy the peace and quiet, the fresh air, and watch the happiness of the ducks as they waddle into their pasture.
- Hearing my kids exclaim like it was Christmas morning that the haskaps are ready to eat and the strawberries have finally turned red.
- Watching a chick excitedly and rather frantically run around with its first worm in its mouth while all the other chicks try to take it from her.
- Relaxing in the shade of the trees to the soft music of the bees' humming as I observe these fascinating creatures come and go from the hive.
- Learning so many new skills that challenge me, scare me, and motivate me to continue on this mud-, manure-, tear-, and sweat-filled adventure.

If you begin your own homesteading journey, I urge you to remember to stop and celebrate these moments … these small successes. (However tiny they may be!) This is what motivated me and what will hopefully encourage you to stick with your farming plans no matter how scary, messy, frustrating, or challenging they may turn out to be.

Inspecting Your Hive

Foraging for Wild Edibles

Cooking from Scratch and in Season

project 20

inspecting your hive

Some homesteading memories will be imprinted in your mind forever. Opening a beehive for your first time is one of them.

The weather was perfect - sunny, warm with just a slight breeze. The bees were humming contentedly as they brought in nectar and tiny sacks of bright orange pollen.

I put on my new, sparkling white bee suit, got all my tools ready, and waited in nervous anticipation for my beekeeping mentor to arrive.

It was time for my first hive inspection.

As I saw George pull into the driveway, I kissed my husband goodbye as if I was going off to war (I may have been worried about being stung to death) and met George outside.

I was excited. I was nervous. I was afraid of being stung. So afraid, in fact, that George had to tell me to quit jerking my hands every time a curious bee came near or I really would get stung. You have to move sloooowly around the bees. Sudden or sharp movements are a recipe for getting stung. If a curious bee does land on you, you can simply blow it away through your veil. Once I realized the bees weren't in the mood to harm me, I started to relax and we got down to beesness.

how often should you inspect your hive?

As a first-time beekeeper, I inspected my hive more often than I should. Why? I wanted to learn how to identify a drone versus a worker bee. I wanted to be able to recognize pollen, nectar, and water. I wanted to practice spotting eggs and larvae. I simply wanted to get a feel for what a normal hive looked like.

But every time you open the hive, you disturb the bees. You may even kill a few. And you will definitely set them back as they will have to repair the propolis seals you've broken and regulate the temperature of the hive.

Therefore, you should only inspect your hive when you have a good reason. For example, you may want to ensure your bees have enough honey for the winter. Or maybe you want to look for signs of swarming.

Once you are more experienced, you may very rarely open your hives. George can tell if something is off just by studying what's going on outside the hive. Tip: This is why it's always a good idea to walk by your hives on a regular basis and spend time observing the bees.

a few things to look for during an inspection

Brood

Have a look at the pattern. Is it indicative of a healthy queen? In this case, there shouldn't be too many empty cells.

Queenlessness

If you can't spot the queen, look for eggs. If you find them, you know your Queen was present within the last three days.

Queen cells

Queen cells are where larvae develop into new queens. These peanut-shaped cells are usually about one inch long and can be found in two different areas depending on why the colony is raising a new queen:

   a. Similar to drone cells, supersedure cells are found on top of the comb. This is a sign that your queen is aging, ill, or missing.

   b. Swarm cells are usually found hanging from the bottom of the frames. In this case, your bees may be producing a new queen to stay in the hive while the current one and half of your bees move to a new home.

Pollen

I panicked when I found a grey substance in some of my cells. It turns out it was just pollen. Pollen comes in many colours including orange, yellow, brown, blue, and even grey.

Nectar or honey in the cells.

Signs of disease, parasites, or pests such as varroa mites.

how to inspect a hive

Normally, you would begin your inspection by preparing your smoker. But as you know from the "how to use a smoker" section, we didn't use one for this inspection. We simply removed the cover and dug in.

supplies

- smoker and lighter, if using
- hive tool
- frame rest, if using

1. Never stand in front of your hive. This is the bees' flight zone and they don't like anyone or anything blocking their entrance. Instead, check your hive from the side.

2. Take a deep breath and remove the roof/outer cover. Place it on the ground.

3. Remove the quilt box or inner cover. If you are using an inner cover, it will likely be stuck to the super with propolis. You'll need your hive tool to pry it off. Try not to let it "pop." The bees will sense the vibrations and become defensive. Always check to make sure the Queen isn't on the inner cover and gently lay the cover on the ground or lean it vertically against the hive.

4. Remove your first frame from the hive. I start with the frame closest to me on the outer wall. It won't be easy to remove. The bees will have "glued" all the frames together. To unstick them, you will need to use the flat end of your hive tool. Insert it between the ends of the first and second frames and twist your tool to separate them. Repeat at the opposite end of the frame.

    If the frame is not too sticky, you might be able to pick it up using your fingers. If it is really stuck, use the curved end of your hive tool to pry it up and then grab each end of the frame firmly by the tabs.

5. Now, standing with your back to the sun so the light can shine deep into the comb, take in the amazing inner life of bees. You may see drones, worker bees, eggs, larvae, nectar, pollen, and if you're lucky — the Queen. Don't forget to check both sides of your frame. Once you're done, place the frame either on the ground leaning vertically against the hive or on a frame rest. Now there is plenty of room in the hive to move the other frames.

6. Grab your hive tool and loosen the second frame. Gently slide it to where the first frame used to be. Check the frame as you did in Step 4, holding it over your super in case any bees fall from the frame, and return it to the hive in the same orientation as before.

7. Work your way through the remaining frames in the same manner.

8. When you're done checking all the frames, slide them back to their original places and replace the first frame you removed. All the frames should now be centred in your super.

9. Replace the inner cover. George showed me a neat trick to ensure you don't smush any bees: Start at one corner and slowly slide the cover across the box. The bees should move out of the way. If, on the other hand, you were to place the cover directly down onto the hive, the bees wouldn't even have a chance to move and you will likely kill a few stragglers hanging on the edges.

10. Replace the outer cover. Now give yourself a pat on the back. This is a skill many people wouldn't even be brave enough to try. You did it!

project 21

foraging for wild edibles

Do you ever get bored with the same old recipes? Me, too.

So what's the solution to a ho-hum meal? Hint: It's in your backyard.

The red clover growing in your grass? Sprinkle the flowers in your salad. The fresh spruce tips on your tree? Toss them in a rice dish or your morning omelette. The wild sorrel flourishing near your garden? Add it to your soup. Spend a little time foraging and your meals will never be boring again.

Best of all — you didn't have to plant them or weed them or water them. These wild, tasty, and nutritious weeds take care of themselves and they're free.

Let's face it. Gardening can be a lot of work so if you can find free food in your yard, you can save yourself time, effort, and money. Sign me up for that! I have been interested in foraging for years. I even attended a few wild edible and medicinal workshops with local experts, but then never harvested a single specimen from my own backyard. LOSER!

So this spring I decided to remedy this. I went on a hunt with the kids to find what I hoped would be all kinds of interesting and delicious morsels. Here's a sample of what we discovered growing wild on the farm.

Lamb's-Quarter (*Chenopodium album* L.)

This weed should really be called "free spinach." It grows wild in my garden and likely in yours too. I strongly encourage you to pick it, but don't even think about throwing it in the compost bin. Lamb's-quarter leaves are delicious freshly picked throughout the summer. Although it tastes similar to spinach, you'd have to eat a lot more spinach to get the same amount of nutrients.

One chopped cup of lamb's-quarter has almost three times the daily recommended intake of vitamin A, more than 100 percent of your daily value of vitamin C, and more than 1,000 percent of your daily recommended intake of vitamin K. Try adding lamb's-quarter to your salad or cook it as you would spinach.

Wild Mint (*Mentha arvensis* L.)

We have more wild mint than we do grass at our farm and it often tries to creep its way into my garden. But I don't complain because I'm looking forward to tasting mint honey from my bees who frequent its purple flowers.

We harvest fresh mint leaves (although the stock is edible too) throughout the summer and throw them into fruit smoothies. The dried leaves also make a soothing tea that helps with digestion. Mint is fairly easy to identify by its square stems, opposite leaves, and, of course, its strong minty smell.

Red Clover (*Trifolium pratense* L.)

Red clover is found in abundance around the farm and is especially loved by my children who pluck the blossoms and suck on the inner part of the sweet flowers.

Although I don't enjoy eating clover by itself, the kids collect the blossoms and I toss them into our morning blueberry pancakes. If you want to get fancy, you can sprinkle the flowers in your salad or use them as a beautiful cake garnish.

Wood Sorrel (*Oxalis acetosella*)

This is hands down our family's favourite weed. Mostly because it tastes like lemon sour candy. You can eat the leaves raw, but I prefer throwing them in salads, sandwiches, and soups for a little extra lemon zing. You can also make a refreshing tea by steeping the leaves in boiling water.

Although this weed is more commonly found in the woods, we discovered it growing among our strawberries. I think I may have overdone it with the wood chips. Even the weeds think it is a forest floor. Wood sorrel is easy to identify by its heart-shaped leaves that grow in groups of three. It typically grows a maximum of 15 inches tall.

Dandelion (*Taraxacum officinale weber*)

Our field turns into a sunburst of dandelions every spring. Their happy yellow heads set against the green grass is a feast for the eyes and our tummies.

Dandelion greens are best picked young before or just after they begin to flower. Otherwise they become bitter. I tried harvesting the leaves and making dandelion fruit smoothies, but it was a complete and bitter flop. However, they are delicious sautéed with butter, vinegar, and garlic or simply add a few petals to your morning omelette.

Although I've never tried it, you can make tea or a coffee substitute with the dried roots and dandelion wine with the flowers.

Plantain (*Plantago major*)

After learning about this common weed during an herb walk with Medical Herbalist Savayda Jarone of Mayflower Herbs Clinic & Dispensary in Halifax, Nova Scotia, I couldn't wait for the next time one of my children injured themselves. I wanted to test out its healing powers. Kidding! Not kidding! Although you can use the leaves in a salad, stir fry, or cup of tea, we use it on the farm as a natural remedy.

You can chew the fresh leaves and apply them directly to the skin as a first-aid remedy for drawing out pus, poison, dirt, splinters, and stings from the skin.

Spruce tips (*Picea* sp.)

You can eat spruce trees? Yes, you can! And yes, I have probably taken foraging a little too far. But, I promise you, the young tips of spruce trees are delicious and they're high in vitamin C and antioxidants. Enjoy them raw or steep the needles to make a tasty tea.

There is a good chance that you too have food growing in your lawn or around your home that you didn't plant and that you probably didn't even know was there. Except for the dandelions. You probably spotted those.

> **CAUTION**
> During both foraging workshops I attended, the instructors warned us to properly identify the plants we were foraging. In many cases, there are lookalikes that could be poisonous.

projects 22 & 23

cooking from scratch and in season

My husband gave me "the look." I had just come back from the garden holding several large bowls overflowing with radishes, some of which had grown to the size of beets.

I had taken succession planting quite seriously. I planted radishes with my carrots, and my beets, and my cucumbers, and my brassicas ... I pretty much sprinkled them in every empty space. The result was a crazy overabundance of radishes. And I had no idea what the heck I was going to do with them. Normally, I might slice one or two in a salad. What was I going to do with bowls of these spicy vegetables?

This was the reason for the strange look my husband was giving me. Let's just say he wasn't as impressed with my radish success, that is until he tasted my solution. Juicy, flavourful roasted radishes! I would have never discovered how delicious radishes are roasted if it weren't for my love of gardening.

The truth is even if I didn't want to learn how to cook from scratch and in season, I really didn't have a choice. This is a skill that will be forced upon you the moment you plant a garden. And that's a good thing. There are so many reasons to learn to cook from scratch and in season from eating healthier to enjoying better tasting food to saving money. So dig out your favourite cookbooks and start dreaming about how you might pickle spring peas, ferment radishes, or whip up a meal using all that extra zucchini.

Beet and Fennel Smoothie

Drawn to its sweet and spicy scent, I planted fennel in my garden. Most likely because I didn't know what I was going to do with it, it quickly grew into a ferny abundance. On a whim, I decided to try a few sprigs in our daily smoothie. It was a delicious success! The subtle hint of black licorice is a tasty addition to this cool, hot pink beverage.

P.S. Save those radish tops! you can sauté them with butter and vinegar and serve as a side dish.

ingredients

- ½ cup water
- 1 cup yogurt
- ½ of a banana
- 1 large beet, peeled and chopped
- a few sprigs of fresh fennel
- 2 cups frozen strawberries

Optional: chop and add the greens from your beet.

instructions

- blend in a high-speed blender until smooth

Honey Custard

If you keep chickens, at some point in your homesteading career, you're going to be faced with an overabundance of eggs. What do you do with them? You make finger-licking-good custard topped with whipped cream. Your eggs will disappear like magic.

ingredients

- 6 eggs
- ½ cup honey (maple syrup is equally delicious
- ½ tsp salt
- 4 cups milk
- 1 tsp vanilla
- 1 tsp cinnamon
- ¼ tsp nutmeg

instructions

- Preheat oven to 350°F. Whisk together eggs and honey and salt.
- Warm milk on medium heat until just below boiling. Slowly whisk the milk into the egg mixture.
- Stir in vanilla and pour into ramekin cups. Top with cinnamon and nutmeg.
- Place ramekin cups in a baking dish filled with hot water to a depth of about an inch.
- Bake for about an hour depending on the size of your ramekin dishes. You'll know they're done when the custard is firm and a wet knife inserted in the centre comes out clean. Cool and top with whip cream. For an even more decadent experience, add a scoop of caramelized apples.

Good Morning Frittata

We eat a lot of eggs (as in four or five dozen a week) because this is one of the few foods we can produce in abundance on our farm. As you begin homesteading, you'll also find yourself eating whatever you can harvest from your backyard. So spend some time searching for interesting recipes featuring these same ingredients so maybe it won't feel like you've had eggs for supper every night of the week.

instructions

- Preheat your oven to 350°F.
- Heat skillet over medium heat and add butter.
- Chop ⅔ of the onion and sauté for about 5 minutes. Add mushrooms.
- Continue sautéing until the onions caramelize.
- Whisk the eggs and water together in a bowl.
- Chop the remainder of the onion.
- Add mushrooms, caramelized onions, spinach, garlic, rosemary, and the finely chopped onions to the egg mixture and pour into your skillet.
- Sprinkle salt, pepper, paprika, and cheese over top and place skillet in the oven until the cheese has melted and the frittata puffs up (about 15 to 20 minutes).

ingredients

- 3 tbsp butter
- 1 large onion
- 1 cup mushrooms, sliced
- 6 eggs
- ¼ cup water
- 1 cup spinach, chopped
- ⅔ tsp garlic, minced
- ½ tbsp fresh rosemary, chopped
- salt, pepper, and paprika to taste
- ½ cup cheddar cheese

Roasted Radishes

It's hard to say what I like most about roasted radishes. It could be their vivid colour or their juicy goodness or the fact that they turn out perfectly every time I make them. Whatever the reason, you haven't really tasted radishes until you've had them roasted. I think you'll be pleasantly surprised by their sweet, mild flavour.

instructions

- Preheat oven to 400°F.
- Coat radishes with olive oil and lemon juice.
- Sprinkle with salt and pepper.
- Arrange the radishes cut-side down in your pan.
- Roast for about 40 minutes.
- Sprinkle with parsley and gobble these juicy morsels up while they're still warm.
- Your life will have changed forever.
- You're welcome.

P.S. Save those radish tops! You can sauté them with butter and vinegar and serve as a side dish.

ingredients

- 20 radishes, trimmed and sliced in half
- 1 tbsp olive oil
- 1 tbsp lemon juice
- salt and pepper, to taste
- 2 tbsp parsley, minced

Mémère's Acadian Chicken Fricot

So simple, so easy to prepare, and so incredibly delicious. If you haven't tasted Acadian Chicken Fricot, you are missing out on some serious soup. You have to, no, MUST, try this recipe. You'll be slurping and smacking your lips in no time.

instructions

- Make a bone broth with the chicken carcass. Simply put the carcass in a pot and cover with water. Let simmer for 24 to 48 hours. Strain out the bones and use the remaining broth for the soup.
- Add the remaining ingredients to the broth. Bring to a boil and then simmer for an hour or until all the vegetables are cooked.
- Eat! And try not to slurp too much.

Note: You may notice that there are not any measurements for how much broth you should use. This is because I just pour enough in to cover the vegetables. Any leftover broth can be frozen and used for your next soup.

ingredients

- One chicken carcass
- 2 or 3 cups of chopped chicken
- 1 large onion, diced
- 8 carrots, peeled and sliced
- 6 large potatoes, peeled and sliced
- 4 celery stalks, sliced
- salt and pepper, to taste
- 1 to 2 tbsp summer savoury spice (no substitutes. This is what makes the soup. Bonus points if you grow your own.)

ingredients

- 6 cups chopped peaches
- 2 tbsp honey
- 1 tsp cinnamon

Peach Rolls Ups

This year I planted a peach tree in hopes that someday I will have hundreds of pounds of fruit to process. But even if that never happens, this recipe will still come in handy. Fruit leather is pricey to buy at the store. Making it at home is cheaper, healthier, and so ... well, kind of easy. OK, it's a little troublesome to make. But it'll be worth it, I promise.

instructions

- Pop your peaches into the freezer for a couple hours and then run them under warm water to easily remove the peel. If you want to impress your friends at your next party, you could show them this trick. In fact, you should all come over to my place for a celebration and I can share a bunch of these really cool party tricks. Wouldn't that be fun? No, really!

- Preheat your oven to its lowest setting. Mine is 170°F. Line a 11x17-inch baking sheet with parchment paper.

- Once thawed, purée the peaches, honey, and cinnamon in a blender until smooth. Pour mixture onto parchment paper and spread to about a ⅛-inch thick. Spread the fruit a little thicker along the edges as it will cook fastest here.

- Place baking sheet in the oven and bake for 8 to 10 hours or until the surface is smooth and no longer sticky.

- While the fruit is still warm, peel off the fruit leather from the parchment paper and cut into strips using a pizza cutter. Roll into parchment paper and store in an airtight container.

JULY

I cried. There was blood dripping down the side of my 6-week-old chick. Sometime during the night, a raccoon had reached through the coop's wire mesh and ripped off one of her wings.

I called the local vet who confirmed my suspicions. She was lucky to be alive. If a human lost an arm, an amputation would be performed, but in the case of a chicken, there wasn't much that could be done — except wait. Because chickens are attracted to blood, it didn't take long for the other chicks to begin pecking at her injury. So we separated the Buff Orpington from her "friends" and put her in a cardboard box with food and water. To my amazement, 20 minutes later she had somehow managed to escape. I found her happily scratching and foraging around the yard. Apparently, she wasn't going to let having just one wing get her down.

With my dad's help we sprayed an antiseptic solution on the wound as the vet recommended (I held the chicken while he, not wanting to see the damage, closed his eyes and sprayed). I added a little infection fighting garlic to her water and hoped for the best. Today, my one-winged wonder chick is still alive and now lovingly nicknamed — Tuff Orpington. We have since learned from this rookie mistake. Our coop, which was made with 1x1-inch wire mesh, is now surrounded by much smaller wire netting. Warning: Don't overestimate the size of a racoon's paw.

This is just one of several challenges we overcame this month. As you know, the chicks were originally housed in our dining room. This was an unfortunate choice as they created a HUGE amount of dust, which we later learned can cause respiratory problems. To combat the dust, we switched from using wood chips as their bedding to soil. Another unfortunate choice. At first, it seemed like a good idea as we were able to grow fresh greens for the chicks by blocking off half of their home until the wheatgrass had a chance to sprout. The chickens also enjoyed scratching in the soil and finding the worms the kids had added.

Unfortunately, it started to smell. And a few days later, the chicks learned to fly to the top of their enclosure. We thought they were so adorable as we enthusiastically applauded their efforts. Until we watched in disgust as they turned their fuzzy butts out over their pen and pooped onto our floor. Their newfound ability to fly also led to several chicks losing their balance and falling onto the floor. Panicked, they would chirp for help until I found the poor things and returned them to their enclosure. And that's when we decided enough was enough. It was time they moved outside.

Embarrassingly, we didn't yet have their coop ready. One of the few benefits of buying a 200-year-old home is they usually come with "bonus" outbuildings — albeit in a questionable state. We had planned to convert one such shed into a coop. But as usual we had jumped into something before we were ready. So, we made a temporary shelter for the chicks with an attached chicken chunnel to control weeds in our garden paths.

To sum up the month, we learned many lessons including one that cost a chick its wing. This book might as well have been called 52 homesteading failures. But I imagine this is how most homesteaders begin their journey. There is just so much to learn, you can't possibly know everything about each and every one of these skills. So you read, you take courses, you find mentors, and then you go out and give it your best try. You may fail. You will make mistakes. And you will learn. You can be sure I would never again use the wrong sized mesh, raise my chicks in my dining room, or jump into a new project before we're ready ... well, actually I may still do that. But, for the most part, from each failure we learn to do it better. And thank goodness for that.

Raising Chicks

Building a Chicken Chunnel

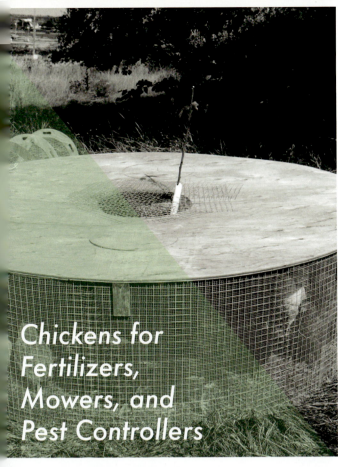

Chickens for Fertilizers, Mowers, and Pest Controllers

Chocolate Mint Strawberry Freezer Jam

How to use a Scythe

project 24
raising chicks

I didn't have an easy time convincing my husband that raising chicks should be part of our challenge. As you may recall, our former chickens lasted for maybe a month before they were all tragically murdered by a raccoon. Of course, this time I assured him it would be different. This time we would build a coop that was impossible for any predator to penetrate.

Alas ... he still wasn't convinced. He argued that we had never raised chicks before. But I mean really ... how hard could it be?

So against his better judgement we ordered 32 heritage chicks from Murray McMurray Hatchery. Why 32? We wanted to sell enough eggs to cover the costs of caring for our chickens so we could eat our eggs for free.

So Jérémie travelled with another local farmer who organized the trip. He was not only picking up chicks for himself, but took orders from many other farmers in the area to cover the cost of driving to and from the U.S.

Jérémie hadn't even brought the day-old chicks home and he was already regretting his decision when halfway to Houlton, Maine, they got a flat tire. So the trip, which was supposed to be a seven-hour drive (including drop offs), turned into an nine-hour ordeal cramped in the car with hundreds of chicks chirping away in the back seat.

Amazingly, every chick survived the journey, and Jérémie was only slightly cranky when he arrived home and found my brilliant cardboard box set up for the chicks in the dining room. I'll admit that this particular crazy idea was all mine.

We ordered our chicks from Murray McMurray Hatchery instead of a local source as they carried many of the dual purpose, heritage breeds we coveted. They were also willing to sex them. If your birds are unsexed, there is a possibility you could end up with 32 roosters, a hard lesson I learned from purchasing our ducks. Half of them turned out to be drakes, and since we hadn't yet worked up the courage to butcher the animals we so lovingly raised, we ended up feeding all the males throughout the winter. This cost us more than planned especially since the ducks decided to stop laying the moment the cold weather hit.

Apparently, they hadn't read the same book as I did, which stated ducks are actually better winter layers than chickens. Not that the chickens could read either. Many sources told me chickens should start laying at 22 weeks. Well, some of them did, but the majority did not. I have a feeling there are a few chickens who hop into a nesting box and then pretend to lay an egg so I never know who might be a candidate for the stew pot. Bird brained? I don't know. I think those chickens are outwitting me.

Choosing a breed

We chose heritage breeds that are suited to our cold climate with small combs and heavy feathering such as the Australorp, Rhode Island Reds, and Buff Orpington. Even our Ameraucaunas with their small comb did well in our Canadian winter, but we choose that breed based on their egg colour.

This was a good business decision as our customers love the different sizes and colours of eggs in every carton — although the first dozen often takes them by surprise. Our Ameraucanas lay beautiful blue/green eggs resulting in all kinds of reactions from "I feel like I should be eating ham with these green eggs," to being jokingly accused of selling robins' eggs, to simply admiring the colourful bounty our chickens provide.

Should you keep a rooster?

If you live in an urban area, you likely won't have a choice and for good reason. Roosters love to crow not only when the sun rises at 5:30 a.m., but at random times throughout the day. And like any good guardian chicken, every time a stranger arrives at the farm.

Our neighbours received notification of our rooster the first time he crowed. Unfortunately, I can't say "Hey Hey" (as he has been unfortunately nicknamed by our kids) is very popular in our neighbourhood.

But we keep him around to help protect the flock. He takes his job seriously, scanning the skies and surrounding area for predators and alerting the flock when they need to seek cover.

However, if you have children, you may have to teach them how to show the rooster who is boss. Hey Hey loves to chase around the kids (possibly in revenge for the name they gave him), but he hasn't done this in a long time. When my daughter sees him start to fluff up his neck feathers to make himself look more ferocious, she picks him up. There is nothing more embarrassing for a macho rooster like Hey Hey than to be cradled and petted and told he is, "a cute little chicky." As soon as she puts him back on the ground, he quickly and rather sheepishly goes back to his chicken business. A few days later he may try again, but eventually he will admit defeat unless provoked.

Bringing your chicks home

As I did for the ducks, I prepared a box filled with wood shavings and reused the Brooder Hen for warmth. Until your chicks are fully feathered, they will huddle under the heat, occasionally leaving in search of food and water.

The only disadvantage with using the Brooder Hen is that unlike the ducks, the chicks hopped on top and pooped. Plan on using some netting to prevent them from making a mess.

Food and water

I had read that chicks can literally drown in their own water so we bought a chick sized waterer — a quart glass Mason jar attached to a stainless steel dish with tiny holes just big enough for them to drink from. We also filled a chick feeder with what's called "chick starter," a slightly higher protein mix than regular feed.

When the chicks are around 8 weeks old, you can switch to a grower mix, and, finally, once they start to lay eggs, you can feed a layer ration, which contains added calcium.

Although we prefer our chickens to eat as natural a diet as possible from food they can forage around our farm, we supplement with organic feed from Backyard Organics in Prince Edward Island.

It would be much cheaper for us to buy non-organic, but we couldn't imagine going through all this trouble just to eat eggs that you can buy for several dollars cheaper at the store. We wanted to provide our family (and community) with the best pesticide- and chemical-free eggs we could possibly produce.

We help lower the cost by fermenting their feed (soaking their feed in water for a few days which, just like fermented foods for humans, makes the nutrients more easily digestible for your birds), sprouting seeds, and feeding them leftover organic kitchen scraps.

The latter is our chicken's favourite food. All I have to do is yell "here, chicky, chicky" and all 32 of my chickens come running from wherever they are in the yard to see what special treat I have for them. Supposedly, there are foods you shouldn't give to your chickens, but mine will eat almost anything except onions and banana peels. They simply won't eat what they don't like. Amazingly, they will devour a whole watermelon including the peel. Chickens really are experts at converting food waste into delicious and nutritious eggs.

If your chicks do not have access to the outdoors, you will also need to supply them with grit. Since chickens do not have teeth, they use tiny rocks to grind their food.

Today, 31 out of 32 chickens are still healthy and, most importantly, alive. (Sadly, one broke her neck. We're still not sure how she managed to do this.) They have been helpful and eager workers on the farm tilling our garden at the end and beginning of the seasons, eating pesky bugs, and keeping weeds out of our garden paths. They make us laugh as they squabble over the best bits of food, sun bathe like divas with their legs fully stretched out behind them, or peek at us through our back door window wondering when their supper will arrive. And they fill our tummies with breakfast every morning. What more could a farm girl want? Get yourself some chickens.

project 25

building a chicken chunnel

How do you control the grass that grows between your garden beds? You get yourself some chickens and you build a chunnel. You will never see weeds in your paths again.

Chickens are tireless workers who love to scratch (it's basically all they do), and in just one day they cleared the path in the photograph opposite to bare dirt.

But that's not all! Chicken chunnels also contain your flock. Currently, we free range our feathered friends, which sounds like a great idea. They can forage for a good part of their own food and they get plenty of exercise and stimulation. But there are hidden challenges with free ranging.

First, if given a choice, your chickens will spend at least some of their time free ranging on your front porch leaving a welcome mat of poo for anyone who comes to visit. On the bright side, this could discourage any unwanted visitors. On the down side, at some point, you're guaranteed to accidentally step in poo right before you hop in your car and wonder … what the heck is that nasty smell?

Your chickens could even decide to free range on top of your car, in your garden, or in the middle of the road. They may even try to free range themselves right into your house because those chickens are no fools. They know where the food and treats come from. At this point, you really don't have a choice but to find a way to contain your wayward flock.

A chunnel will still allow your birds to eat weeds and bugs without wreaking havoc in your yard. Bonus: Unlike a fence, the chunnel also protects the chickens from aerial predators.

To build a secure chicken chunnel, you need a four-foot wide roll of 16 gauge, ½-inch, galvanized wire mesh. It can be as long as you want, but you will have to attach it to a wooden base so it should be a length that's easy to find in lumber. We chose 12 feet. (Beware when cutting the mesh as the edges can be sharp. Use gloves or don't say I didn't warn you!)

- Cut 1½ inches from two 12-foot pieces of 1x3 and lay them down parallel four feet apart. With the help of another person, start laying the mesh down leaving it overhang at least ¾ of an inch over the wood at the beginning and ends. As you go along unrolling the mesh, staple it down to the wood.

- Once completed, screw down two uncut 12-foot pieces of 1x3 to sandwich and secure it. This added security will prevent raccoons from ripping those pesky staples out. It also creates a ledge to easily secure the frame to the ground.

- The wood should be exterior grade or stained to protect it.

- Once you're done, you need to make the ends. They will be used to shape the chunnel and double as end caps if needed.

- The ends will be about 22 inches wide by 18¾ inches tall, cut into an oblong shape. You can use ¾-inch plywood or fasten thin scrap wood together.

Once you cut one, and double-check that it fits the wire, copy it onto another. You could also do the layout on Bristol board and transfer the pattern. The critical part is simply to make sure the perimeter is 48 inches.

• Next, find the middle of the wire mesh and with a large, flat washer and screws, affix it to the top of your cut outs. Then continue attaching the mesh along the perimeter to create your shape. If you plan on moving the chunnel, I recommend installing a minimum of three cross pieces on the bottom of the frame to keep everything solid.

• That's it.

• Since our chickens were housed overnight in our chunnel, we cut old wire shelving that we happened to have on hand and stuck them in the ground along the edges to prevent predators from digging underneath. Whatever fasteners you have available can be used. Just make sure you use them.

Although this design is predator proof, it's not permanent. Depending on the amount of chickens you have, it should be moved on a regular basis.

Now all you have left to do is sit back and watch your chickens do your weeding.

project 26

chickens for fertilizers, mowers, and pest control

We don't mow — ever. This was fine when we lived in a forest, but now we live amongst grass and hayfields. And yet we still don't mow, partly because we never seem to have enough time and partly because the lawn becomes a meadow for bees and fodder for animals. This is great — except when you're planting fruit trees that can't compete with grass.

So, until our sheep arrived, Jérémie came up with another solution — a movable chicken coop that can surround a tree. In just 15 minutes, you can have this coop disassembled from one tree and reassembled around another.

Here are the criteria he used to come up with a solution:

- Environmentally and physically less energy intensive
- Materials that are not only recyclable and long-lasting, but biodegradable.
- A design that would benefit our trees and get rid of, or at the very least, keep the pesky voles at bay.
- Help lower our chicken feed costs in hopes that the system would pay for itself in a few years.

So off to the drawing board (well, actually, it was a piece of cardboard ripped from a chicken feed bag but you get the idea) he went.

The design was simple and basic. Now you may be wondering why is it round? To save space and money. A round design would give him the most amount of space using the least amount of fencing material (the costliest part of the design).

supplies

- 25 feet of 2-foot-wide ½-inch square galvanized wire mesh
- 2 sheets of ½-inch plywood
- screws
- exterior grade glue
- skill saw
- jig saw
- wire cutters

In the photographs (Page 127), you can see he used 2-foot-wide 1-inch square galvanized wire mesh because that's what we had on hand. However, since the "One Winged Wonder Chick" incident, Jérémie decided to add a second layer of ¼-inch mesh. He tied them together with steel wire at every foot on the bottom and the top. But if he were to do it again, he'd opt for the 2-foot wide ½-inch square galvanized wire mesh as it would save a lot of time.

instructions

1. To create the roof of the movable coop, put together two sheets of ½-inch plywood. Find the center and scribe an eight-foot circle on the exterior perimeter of the plywood.

2. Scribe three smaller 18-inch circles. One circle should be placed in the middle between the two plywood pieces and two more at approximately 24 inches up at 90 degrees from the center of the long edge of each 8-foot semi-circle piece.

3. Cut the circles out with a jigsaw being extra careful when cutting the two full 18-inch circles as those pieces will be used later as lids. These two openings will allow you to easily provide your chickens with food and water.

4. Create a lip on the straight edge of one of the plywood semi circles by attaching two pieces of wood measuring 1 by 4 inches by 35 inches long. Stop approximately four inches short from the outside ends. This lip will act as a support for the other large plywood semi circle that will be screwed on when putting it together to create the roof.

5. We also used small leftover pieces of mesh and wood to fill in the area between the tree trunk and the plywood. This would need to be adjusted for every tree. To support the two lids that will be used to access the feed and water, add two small lips parallel to each other on both sides underneath the plywood. This will allow the lids to rest flush with the plywood. You may want to install a handle or drill a hole that will allow you to more easily remove the lid.

6. One way to put it all together is to rest the two large plywood pieces on the ground with the tree in the middle. Then unroll the wire mesh so it runs the perimeter. Remove the plywood pieces now overlapping the fence end by about nine inches and replace the plywood on top.

7. Add a wooden u-shaped end to hug the mesh tight and a small door in the wire mesh so you can gather your chickens into a moveable chicken chunnel before disassembling and then reassembling the unit around the next tree. You could also use the opening to connect multiple units together using temporary chicken chunnels.

Although this design worked, we did discover one problem. There isn't a space for your chickens to roost. You would have to expand upwards unless you used this system with meat chickens or, as in our case, your chickens are still young.

Just like the chicken chunnel, this system isn't permanent. You must move it from tree to tree every few days as it won't take long for your chickens to fertilize the area and scratch away anything that dare grows. If you used this system in the early spring, your chickens would also take care of any overwintering pests. Bonus!

project 27

chocolate mint strawberry freezer jam

It was the chocolate's fault. It was the reason I rushed home excitedly from our local garden store to show the kids the cool, new herb we'd be planting in our garden — chocolate mint.

If you are a chocolate lover (and who isn't?), you understand my need to purchase and eat anything chocolate. It smelled heavenly. It looked harmless. I planted it.

Now I knew mint was invasive. And I've heard a billion times that you should always plant it in a container. But I didn't. It smelled like chocolate mint patties. What could go wrong?

So I planted that innocent looking herb right into the ground thinking how I would just keep an eye on it. I really thought that if it grew too big, I'd harvest large bundles and dry them to make chocolate mint tea or hot cocoa.

That was before I knew chocolate mint was evil. It secretly planned and dug a series of elaborate tunnels under the ground only to reappear on the opposite side of the garden and then creep its way around the entire area. I spent days picking it out. I hate chocolate mint.

But I love jam … so I got my sweet revenge in the form of strawberry chocolate mint strawberry freezer jam. (FYI: I've learned my lesson and the evil plant now sits contained in a pot.)

Why freezer jam?

When you're short on time and you just happen upon quarts and quarts of local strawberries on sale for a ridiculous price, freezer jam is your answer.

When it's late at night and you're exhausted from working in the garden and really just want to relax, freezer jam is the solution.

When your two children decide they want to "help" you make jam and you're starting to lose your patience, freezer jam comes to the rescue.

In summary, when you need to make jam fast — think freezer jam.

I was actually planning on water bath canning until the kids decided they wanted to take part. Since freezer jam is easier and quicker to make, I decided we might as well learn a new skill.

Compared to water bath canning there are many other benefits. Since you don't have to use sugar as a preservative, you can use a lot less sweetener in freezer jam. In fact, I only used honey.

Second, the freezer seems to better preserve the authentic, fresh taste of those summer berries.

Finally, although we used the traditional glass canning jars, you can use whatever containers you like since they don't have to be sealable.

The only downside to freezing jam is there's likely only so much room in your freezer.

This recipe is a little different than your typical freezer jam. I wanted to experiment with using natural pectin from apples instead of the store-bought, packaged version. It worked, but resulted in a runnier, although definitely just as tasty, jam. Let's just say there were no leftover jars by winter's end.

I also experimented with adding chocolate mint from my garden, which you can omit if you prefer plain and simple strawberry jam.

This recipe is for all my fellow beekeepers who are always looking for more ways to use honey, those of you who like to use natural sweeteners instead of sugar, and anyone wondering what to do with all that chocolate mint.

ingredients

- 6 lbs hulled and sliced strawberries (minus a few that I ate)
- 3 cups shredded Granny Smith apples, with skins
- 1½ tbsp lemon juice
- 1½ cups honey
- 1½ tbsp finely chopped chocolate mint (optional)

 NOTE If you like a thick jam, use store-bought pectin instead of apples. I wanted to try a natural thickener and, although it works, the end result is definitely runnier.

instructions

1. Mash the strawberries and combine with apples and lemon juice in a large pot. Bring to a boil.

2. Reduce heat and stir in honey and very finely chopped mint. Simmer for about 30 minutes or until the jam has thickened. Warning: This recipe does not become as thick as typical store-bought jam made with pectin. See my note above in the ingredient list.

3. Allow to cool and then ladle into freezer-safe containers leaving about an inch of headspace at the top of your jar or you could end up with a mess in your freezer to clean.

This project really was just as easy as the three steps I described above. So easy my kids could work right alongside me. In fact, if you are just beginning to preserve foods, I would recommend starting with freezer jam for this reason.

project 28

how to use a scythe

Did you know you can harvest an acre of hay or grain in just one day using a scythe? Well, at least once you get the hang of it. On our small acreage, this simple tool could save us from spending big bucks on equipment. So, when we saw a used one for sale, we snagged that deal before hundreds of others could pick it up. OK, in reality, there wasn't anyone else interested. But still, it was exciting.

My husband got his hands on the new toy first and used it to trim around our fruit trees and bushes, and clear the overgrown grass under our fences — all without having to burn fossil fuels or breathe in a single toxic fume from the lawnmower.

Our plan is to be able to hand cut enough grass over the summer to dry into winter hay for our sheep. Any excess will be used as garden mulch.

As a bonus, if you're into yoga or meditation, a scythe may be a handy addition to your routine. The repetitive rhythm and soft swish of the blades is strangely relaxing. Hmmm ... Maybe I'll start a group scything class at the farm. Now there's a novel of way of earning an income from your homesteading activities and getting someone else to cut your hay.

Now if you're using the scythe correctly, like my husband, it actually doesn't take nearly as much effort as you might think. But my experience was not as meditative. I was huffing and puffing, and swinging that scythe like it was a golf club until I was sweating and my arms hurt.

I'm assuming my husband was having a good chuckle as he watched me. Only later did he point out there was an easier way to use the scythe. Although I am certainly not an expert, here are few tips to help you get started:

1. First, sharpen your blade often and definitely every time you use it. It will only cut effortlessly through the grass if it is razor sharp.

2. Make sure your scythe is properly adjusted for your height.

3. Turn with your torso, not your arms — or else you will tire yourself out quickly. This is more of a workout for your legs and torso rather than your arms.

4. Keep the blade on the ground during the forward and return strokes. Read this again. You are NOT holding it off the ground like you see me doing in the photo. I have since learned from this rookie mistake.

5. Start with your blade on your right side (assuming you are right handed) with your right foot forward. Slice in a sweeping arc in front of you and over to your left side while shifting your weight from the right leg to the left.

6. Be gentle with your scythe. Do not swing it around like I did my first try. You'll not only tire yourself out, but the blade can dent, bend, or break.

7. The scythe works more efficiently on wet grass so consider mowing in the cool of the morning.

   So far, I've calculated I can harvest ZERO acres with a scythe. Let's just say that developing this skill takes time, patience, and practice. You will either find it is the perfect cutting tool or that you really need to buy a tractor.

AUGUST

I bought a gym for my bees. Yes, you read that right. But no, they're not exercising their little bee biceps or working out their legs on a mini bee treadmill. They are fighting vampires (varroa mites) — tick sized parasites that feed on their blood. The bees can scrape the mites off their backs and stomachs using the Bee Gym's clever wires and flippers.

Most beekeepers use chemical treatments to take care of the mites, but I wanted a natural solution. I admit the Bee Gym sounded almost too good to be true, but some beekeepers had already had success with the new tool so I thought I'd test it out despite the protestations from my mentor who felt I should learn to manage my colony before getting into exotic beekeeping devices.

This is great advice that you should take. Unfortunately, I didn't. Now the package said you could place the Bee Gym on top of your bottom board or in a spacer on top of your brood box. Well, I chose to use a spacer and what a BIG mistake that was. Although a spacer would have worked fine in the winter when it's too cold for the bees to build comb, using a spacer was a terrible idea in August.

The bees taught me a lesson I will never forget. Any time you violate the bee's space, they will fill it with burr comb. What is burr comb? When you visit your hive, you may find bits of comb built in odd places.

For example, on the underside of your cover or, as in this case, inside your spacer. When this happens, you simply scrape it away and bring it inside with dreams of candles, lip balm, and lotions dancing in your head. Eventually, you will end up with a pile of comb that you can render into beeswax. Of course, my pile shouldn't be as large as you see in the picture on Page 132. This is due to the Bee Gym beekeeping mistake I just described.

Just before we were supposed to go on vacation, I discovered the bees had built comb onto the bottom of each of the eight frames in both of my hives — something they would have never been able to do without the extra room my spacer gave them.

If the comb would have been empty, it wouldn't have been a big deal, but they had filled its cells with larvae, nectar, and pollen. I did not want to scrape it away, but what choice did I have? The heart crushing job had to be done despite the fact that we were supposed to be meeting relatives in Saint John in a couple hours. So we put our plans on hold and began the hardest homesteading task of the entire year. It was a sad and depressing job as we watched the nurse bees try unsuccessfully to save the babies.

Or so we thought. Later, George explained the bees most likely would have only raised drone (male bees) brood along the bottom of the frames. Varroa actually prefer to reproduce in drone cells. By removing the comb before they hatched, we were likely removing many of the mites — significantly reducing the number of them in the colony. We may have accidentally done the bees a favour.

We also left the comb outside their hive so they could salvage the nectar and pollen from the cells. Eventually, I brought the comb inside so as not to attract other robbing insects to the hive. So what did I do with the comb? I certainly didn't let it go to waste. Comb is a precious substance. Bees have to visit millions of flowers, fly around the world about 13 times, and use roughly six pounds of honey just to produce one pound of wax.

So this month I learned how to render my honeycomb into clean and pure beeswax, which I used to make honey hand salve and peppermint lip balm. Sadly, this wasn't the end of my beekeeping adventures. I think the bees were angry with me after the Bee Gym incident. So it's not surprising that half of my bees decided they had had enough of me and were leaving the hive I had bought for them. But I was smarter — or so I like to think. Because I caught those trouble-making bees and put them in a new home where I could keep a close watch on their sneaky behaviours.

P.S. I do still use the Bee Gym, which is now located on the bottom of my hive. I haven't had any further problems. But does it work? I haven't been using it long enough to know. However, I will update my website (theoldwalshfarm.com) with my findings.

The Great Bee Escape

Finding the Queen Bee

Honeycomb into Beeswax

Honey Hand Salve

Lip Balm

Harvest Your Honey

project 29

the great bee escape

This was NOT supposed to be one of the 52 skills I learned this year. My bees were NOT supposed to try and run away from home. And so I wasn't prepared when, much to my horror and dismay, I discovered a bee swarm perched more than 20 feet high in our Maple tree. I'll be honest. I completely panicked. I knew I needed help and I was extremely fortunate my uncle, Ernie Steeves, lived nearby.

Unfortunately, he didn't have any more experience with a bee swarm than I did. But he wasn't worried. He had watched a YouTube video explaining how to do it. A VIDEO. We were going to catch the bee swarm based on the instructions from a YouTube special.

I knew this wasn't good. But what choice did I have? I had a bee swarm in my front yard and I needed to get them in a hive fast before they moved on to their unknown-to-me destination and I lost them — and my investment. So I thanked Ernie for his help (I owe you BIG TIME), and we hatched up a plan. Are you ready for this highly thought out, well developed strategy?

Here it goes: Ernie was going to climb a ladder to cut the branch the bees were resting on. I was to stay on the ground and catch the branch. That's right. I was going to catch a falling bee swarm. This just proves how badly I wanted to get my bees back. And yes, I did have doubts about our plan and yes, I reeeaaaally wished I was the one cutting the branch. But hey, beekeeping is not for the faint of heart. As they say, "Your passion better burn brighter than your fears." So I thanked my lucky stars that I had invested in the full body bee suit and mentally prepared myself for the worst. The good news is I caught the branch.

The bads news is there was an accident mid-air and about 90 percent of the bees fell to the ground in a giant, buzzing puddle. Only a few, well-attached stragglers remained on the branch I was holding. Of course, this didn't happen on the YouTube video. So we resorted to improvisation. Ernie had an empty hive he had brought over. We tipped it on its side next to the bees, prepared to brush, shovel, or scoop them inside. But we didn't have to do any of that. As if by magic, they all started to make their way into the hive.

You may now call me "The Bee Whisperer." I'm thinking of starting a swarm catching sideline business. What do you think? Today, I still have three hives. I was fortunate and those rogue bees decided to stay put in their new home. But this isn't always the case. I am told that after you catch a swarm, the bees can still decide to leave the hive up until they have mature brood (baby bees). This can take a week so it's best not to disturb the hive before then.

I am also now much more educated on bee swarms. Let me now fill you in on some of the blanks in my story.

Why did the bees swarm?

It is most likely because I wasn't quick enough to give them another super. The bees may have felt like they were running out of room and decided to solve the problem by swarming.

What happens when the bees swarm?

Half of your bees leave the hive with the Queen. The remaining bees raise a new queen and stay put in the hive.

Is there a better way to catch a swarm?

One of my beekeeping readers suggested a much easier method using a pail on a pole. Simply slip the bucket up and under the bees. You can then use the pole to poke the branch hard enough so the bees fall into the bucket. Now all you have to do is pour them into your hive. If the Queen is in the box, the stragglers will follow.

He also suggested spreading an old blanket under your super. This is a much easier surface for your bees to walk on than grass.

Why do you think the bee swarm went willingly into the hive?

Although I wish I had some kind of bee superpower, it is mostly likely because the queen had fallen into the box and the other bees were following her. As long as you catch the Queen, you've caught the whole swarm. So if you catch a swarm and they all fly out of the hive, it is likely you didn't get the Queen. Keep trying.

Why didn't the bees attack you?

Bee swarms are almost always docile. Why? I'm not sure. I've read it is because they are so full of honey stores, they can't be bothered. You know how

you feel after second helpings of Christmas dinner? I've also heard it is because they have nothing (brood, honey, home) to defend.

So now that I've successfully caught a bee swarm, if you happen to need one removed from your area, you can give me a call and I'll help. I'll climb up the ladder and cut the branch they are hanging from and you can stay on the ground and catch them. Sound good?

Note: The uncle in this story is not my biological uncle, but my childhood best friend's uncle. However, I've called Ernie uncle ever since I can remember. Today, he is also my brave and helpful neighbour who keeps bees and enjoys watching YouTube videos.

project 30
finding the queen bee

I was worried. Even though everything I had read pointed to the fact that my Queen was likely still alive, what if in the commotion of catching my escaped bees, she died? Without a Queen my whole colony was dead.

Without the Queen, there was no way for my bees to make a new one in their new hive filled with empty frames. So I needed to find my Queen. But ...

Do you really need to find the Queen?

Mostly likely, no. If you see eggs, then you know the Queen was on duty at least 3 days ago. Of course, honey bee eggs are tiny. They are about 1 to 1½ millimeters long, which is approximately half the size of a grain of rice. If you can't see the eggs, look for larvae — pearly white, slug-like (sorry, bees!), C-shaped forms in the cells. Larvae only stays uncapped for about eight days so if you can see those baby bees, you know the Queen was alive and well at least eight days ago. In case you are wondering ... it takes 21 days to go from fertilized egg to worker bee.

However, in my case, I did want to confirm my Queen was alive and maybe you have a good reason too. Perhaps you're splitting your hive (making a second bee colony from your existing beehive usually to prevent swarming) or maybe you just want to impress visitors to your farm with your Queen finding skills.

FUN FACT The Queen is the only bee who can lay fertile eggs. She lays between 1,500 and 2,000 eggs a day. Long live the Queen! See, wasn't that fun?

TIP To help you find honey bee eggs, buy yourself a pair of reading glasses and wear them when you inspect the hive. Then hold your frame so the sun shines into the bottom of the cells and you should be able to easily spot them.

Marked versus an unmarked Queen – and what the heck is that?

First of all, spotting the Queen among 40,000 other bees who look almost identical is tricky, but it's even more difficult when you have an "unmarked Queen." (A "marked Queen" has a dab of paint on the top centre of her thorax.) Without that marking, it is REALLY hard for newbies like myself to find the Queen. It's like "Where's Waldo" every time you open the hive — only Waldo moves and there is always the chance you might get stung, which makes it way more exciting than the traditional game. But it's not impossible to find her and it's a good skill to learn because ... guess what? The mark on the Queen can wear off, another bee could hide the mark from your view or, just like my colony, they could swarm and the old hive will raise a new, unmarked Queen.

How to check your hive to find the Queen bee

I always check my hives starting with the outermost frame. After removing that very first outer frame, always ensure the Queen isn't on it and then you can set it aside or place it on a hive rack. A hive rack isn't necessary (you can set your frames sideways against the side of your hive instead). But I prefer a hive rack because I'm clumsy. With my luck, I'd knock the frame over with my foot.

By setting aside the first frame, you have more room to work so you don't accidentally smush the Queen bee as you inspect the other frames. As you look over the other frames, place each one back in the hive, leaving a space between the ones you've checked and haven't checked so the Queen can't go where you've already inspected.

Look for frames with brood

I was told by my mentor that my Queen would likely be in the middle of one of the centre frames that contains brood (baby bees). Spoiler alert — that is exactly where I found her. Of course, always check both sides of the frames before gently putting each one back down into the hive.

Warning: The Queen can move quickly

The Queen will often dart towards the dark side of the frame. So you'll have to learn to do this quickly. But this can also work to your advantage.

Look for something out of the ordinary

As the Queen crawls around, the other worker bees will move out of her way except for her own entourage of maids who feed and care for her every need. The Queen's only job is to lay eggs. So you may notice a circle of bees surrounding another bee. Take a closer look because you've probably just found your Queen.

Don't drop the Queen on the ground

When checking your frames, always hold them

above your boxes so if the Queen falls, she doesn't land on the ground. You want her to fall right back in the hive.

What does the Queen look like?

First, she is bigger or at least longer and narrower than any other bee in the hive. At first, I kept mistaking the male bees (drones) for the Queen as they are bigger than the numerous female worker bees. The difference is that drones have big eyes and a large, blunt body whereas the Queen is long with a tapered hind end allowing her to reach the bottom of the cells when she lays eggs.

Finding your Queen takes practice — one of the reasons new beekeepers often have to check their hives more often than an experienced beekeeper. I can't say I'm an expert because it still takes me forever scanning my eyes back and forth in rows across each and every frame, but with a little time, I can spot her. And yes, I still get excited and give out a loud, nerdy beekeeper squeal each time I find her.

project 31

honeycomb into beeswax

You're cool. That's what my 8-year-old daughter told me as she watched me render bits of honeycomb into beeswax. I am writing this down so I can remind her of this fact when she becomes a know-it-all teenager who is embarrassed of her homesteading mama.

But I have to admit, she was right. OK, maybe I'm not cool, but what I was doing certainly was. There is something Harry Potterish about experimenting with rendering comb into beeswax and then mixing together different combinations of butters, oils, and fragrances. It felt like a Hogwarts' activity, and I'm convinced the resulting hand salve will work magic on your dry hands.

supplies

- cheesecloth
- clips, twist ties, or rubber bands
- large old pot
- old pair of tongs

instructions

- Wrap your bits of honeycomb in a piece of cheesecloth and clip or tie it tightly closed.

- Fill your old pot halfway with water. (I can't stress the word "old" enough. Your pot will be almost impossible to clean afterwards.)

- Heat the water to medium/low. Do not boil. Beeswax is highly flammable.

- Place your honeycomb bundle into the pot. As the water heats, the beeswax will melt and seep out of the cheesecloth leaving any debris inside the cloth.

- Once it seems like all the wax has melted, you can remove the cheesecloth from the pot giving it one last squeeze with a pair of tongs to get any remaining wax out.

- In just a couple hours, the beeswax will have formed a solid layer on top of the water. Press down gently to remove it and voilà!

You are now ready to turn beeswax into whatever product you can dream up. You could try making mustache cream or surgical bone wax or use it to fashion your dreadlocks. Or maybe just make hand salve.

project 32

the best honey hand salve

How can I say this is THE best hand salve? Because you are going to make it with YOUR favourite ingredients in a combination that best suits YOUR skin.

ingredients

- Beeswax: I used a consistency of 1 part beeswax to 4 parts oil. If you would like a softer salve, add more oil. If you would like a harder salve, use more wax. You may have to experiment to determine the best consistency for your skin.

- Oils: Coconut oil seems to be the latest darling of the beauty world, but I prefer extra virgin olive oil. It doesn't clog my pores, works wonders on my dry skin, and is easily absorbed. I combined the olive oil with another rich, skin strengthening oil — jojoba. It has natural anti-inflammatory properties, as well as microbacterial properties that are healing for the skin, according to OTC Beauty Magazine: "This oil can be used to treat acne, sunburn, and psoriasis." If you don't like olive or jojoba, you can also substitute coconut, sweet almond, avocado, or whatever your favourite oil may be.

- Honey: I added a dash of honey to my salve for its healing and antimicrobial properties.

- Essential oils: Not only do essential oils smell amazing, each one has unique properties that could improve your skin. I love the scent of lavender and since I'm prone to getting cuts and scrapes from working with my hands, I benefit from its healing properties. Of course, there are many other skin friendly essential oils including calendula, geranium, patchouli, sandalwood, and many more. Choose your favourite.

instructions

To make the hand salve, melt the wax and oil on low heat while continuously mixing your brew. Remove from heat and add honey and essential oils. Pour into your containers to set. And there you have it. An inexpensive, all natural, ultra moisturizing alternative to store-bought hand salve, which you are never going to buy again. Right?

project 33

homemade lip balm

I timed it. You can make your own all natural, luxurious, homemade lip balm in less than 15 minutes. I have a hard time just getting dressed and putting on lip balm in 15 minutes.

And do you know how much it cost to make homemade lip balm? Less than $2. Last year, I bought a similar sized container for $5.

This all natural lip balm is not only cheaper than almost anything store bought, but so much better. In fact, I believe it works miracles. My lips are so sensitive that I can't wear most lipsticks, and even some lip balms on the market end up irritating instead of soothing them. But I have been wearing this balm for months and my lips have never been better.

If you suffer from chapped lips or are simply a crazy lip balm lover like me, I urge you to give this recipe a try. Just one word of caution. Be careful how much you make. If stored in a cool, dry place, your lip balm should last a year. Keep this in mind when you're buying your supplies.

If you are like me, you could get so excited about this project and the potential of making your own lip balm that you order 200 lip balm tubes and five pounds of shea butter from Amazon. Fortunately, homemade lip balm makes a great Christmas gift.

supplies & ingredients

- small saucepan
- small glass jar
- measuring spoon
- 4 tsp beeswax
- 2 tsp shea butter
- 5 tsp sweet almond oil (or olive or grapeseed oil)
- stirring stick
- ¼ tsp essential oil of your choice
- lip balm containers (pots, tubes, whatever you fancy)

instructions

1. Fill your saucepan with about 1 inch of water and bring to a boil.

2. Combine beeswax, shea butter and almond oil in the small glass jar.

3. Bring the temperature down to low and set your jar into your pan. Stir until the wax and butter have melted.

4. Add your essential oil and mix vigorously to combine.

5. This is the hardest step. Remove your jar from the pot and quickly (but carefully) pour the melted lip balm into those tiny tubes. You have to work fast as the liquid will begin to turn solid as soon as it cools.

Your lip balm should harden and be ready to use within 10 to 20 minutes. And you're done! Now don't be surprised if your lip balm suddenly disappears. The kids love having their own lip balm (and then losing it) and even Jérémie has decided this lip balm is manly enough for him to carry around. So maybe you do want to buy that package of 200 containers.

project 34 & 35

remove honey filled frames and harvest honey

Wait a second, Kimberlee. You said you didn't harvest any honey from your hives in your first year. You got me! Just like most first-year beekeepers, my bees weren't strong enough to make enough to share. They needed every drop just to make it through the winter.

But my hopes are high for the second summer. Surely, I will need to know how to harvest gallons and gallons of honey from my hives. So my mentor, George, let me tag along at his apiary for an afternoon of removing honey supers and later I was able to watch him extract the honey from the frames.

Now this is a homesteading skill I could do all day long … mostly because I can sneak spoonfuls of honey (and only the bees will know)! Of course, before you can enjoy that honey, you have to get rid of the bees — unless you like a little extra protein with your sugar.

To do this, George installs what's called a Quebec-style "bee escape board" beneath the honey supers he wishes to remove a day or two before harvest time. The bee escape is a clever device that allows the bees to go down into the bottom boxes of the hive, but they can't easily figure out how to travel back up. Of course, the bees are quite clever too and if the bee escape is left on for more than a couple days, the bees may solve the puzzle and make their way back into the supers.

Normally, if you return to your hive within a day or two after installation, there shouldn't be any bees left in your supers. Unfortunately for George, there were still some stragglers due to the warm weather. In cool temperatures, the bees will cluster in the bottom boxes. If not, they will likely stay put beside their precious nectar.

Now what? You can simply remove each of the frames one by one, gently brush the bees off with a damp bee brush (ensure you shake off any excess water) and place the frames in a new box. Don't forget to put a cover over your box or the bees will fly back in as fast as you take them out.

This method would probably work well if you only had one or two hives, but if you have 70 hives, as in George's case, you might want to invest in a bee blower, which operates much like a leaf blower. In fact, George uses a leaf blower.

Basically, a stream of air blows the bees off the comb much like being tossed in the wind. As long as they are not propelled into a solid object, the bees remain unharmed and can simply fly back to their hive or go off in search of their honey box. I was impressed at how fast and efficient this method was versus having to manually go through each frame.

Here's how a bee blower works:

1. Remove your honey super and turn it onto its side on top of your hive so the top of the box is facing you.

2. Turn on your machine and move the nozzle up and down between each frame until all the bees have been removed.

○ **NOTE** You should only harvest frames that are at least three quarters capped. If not, your honey will ferment. However, there is an exception. Sometimes the bees just haven't had a chance to cap the honey. Perhaps there is lots of nectar available so instead of expending energy capping the frames, the bees will send extra troops out to gather food. You can test whether a frame is ready to harvest by holding onto both sides and giving it a good shake. If nothing comes out, the honey is cured and can be extracted.

How to use an extractor:

Now the real fun begins! It's time to bring your supers to your honey house. I have had the pleasure of visiting three such houses and dream of having my own one day with shelves to store my equipment, a couple lounge chairs to relax in while I slurp on my honey, and, of course, my centrifuge honey extractor. This device has a complicated name, but I assure you, it is actually a very simple piece of equipment.

Basically, it is a steel drum that will hold several of your frames in a basket of sleeves. When the drum spins, honey is flung out of the combs and drips down the inside walls of the extractor and out of a spout at the bottom and into your collection bucket or jar.

instructions

1. If you can, extract your honey while it's still warm and the room temperature is around 85°F. This allows the honey to flow more easily.

2. Place a strainer and your bucket or jar under the extractor's closed spout.

3. Uncap your honey. You can do this by gently sliding the blade of a warm knife (you don't want it to be too hot or you'll burn your honey) across your frames to remove the cappings (wax seals). Do both sides.

4. Insert the uncapped frames into your extractor. Try to place them so the weight on all sides of the extractor is equally distributed. If it's unbalanced, your extractor will bounce and move around and your honey may not extract properly.

5. Turn on the machine or, if you have a less expensive manual model, roll up your sleeves and put your muscles to work cranking the handle. The extractor will spin the honey from the comb — leaving the comb intact. I point this out because this is a huge benefit for the bees who won't have to rebuild the comb when you reuse the frames in your hive. Now, there are two main types of honey extractors — tangential and radial. Tangential machines have one side of the combs facing outwards, which means you'll have to spin your machine for about five minutes and then stop and check to see if the comb is empty. If so, you have to switch the orientation of the frames to expose the other side. You would then spin for another five minutes. By this time, the comb on both sides of the frames should be empty. George uses a radial extractor. In this case, the top bar of the frame is facing outwards. Although more expensive than a tangential extractor, it flings honey out of both sides of the frame at the same time so you only have to load your frames once.

6. You can now open the spout and watch as your honey flows through the filter and into your bucket.

Can't afford an extractor? Try this instead.

First, scrape the comb from your frames and into a container. Next, crush the comb until there are no chunks left. Finally, strain the honey over a large pot or bucket and let sit overnight. In the morning, your honey should have dripped down into your pot and most of the wax should still be in your strainer. Or, you can save yourself the work of crushing the comb and simply bottle the raw chunks in a jar. You just may become addicted to the chewy combination of honey and comb.

You must now take a meditative moment to savour a heaping spoonful (or three, or four, or five) while considering yourself the world's luckiest homesteader. Life on the farm will never be sweeter. Give thanks to the bees and enjoy your hard-earned reward.

TIP Instead of using a knife to uncap your honey, try using a capping scratcher to remove the wax seals. But instead of "scratching," peel or skim the wax seals. If you scratch, you'll find pieces of wax in your extractor, which will clog the filter.

DID YOU KNOW It takes 36 pounds of honey to draw out the 10 frames of comb in a deep super. If you cut away the comb every time you harvest your honey, the bees will have to gather another 36 pounds of honey just to remake the comb.

SEPTEMBER

This was the month we grabbed our pitch forks, put on our superman capes, and began our 52 homesteading skills in a year challenge.

How did I come up with the idea? It all started at lunch one day several years ago when a former colleague of mine asked, "If you didn't have any bills to pay and could do anything you wanted, what would you do?" What was my answer? You guessed it — I would start a small farm.

Everyone at the table had a good chuckle including me. Yeah, what a silly idea. Me, who knows nothing about farming.

"No, really," they asked. "What would you do? Wouldn't you want to move to the Bahamas, relax and sit on the beach all day?" Actually, I would. For maybe 23 minutes. And then my fair skin would burn to a crisp and I'd be headed to the local real estate office to find out how I could purchase farmland in the Caribbean.

Despite my homesteading dreams, I likely would have stayed at my communications job forever. The work was enjoyable, the pay was good, and the people I worked with were awesome. But then I got pregnant. That's when I started thinking more about what was really in the food I was buying at the store and how the meat I was eating had been raised. I started having concerns about the environment and what the world of my children and grandchildren would look like.

It wasn't long before my nightstand, which used to be crowded with the latest fiction, was now overflowing with titles such as "The Resilient Farm and Homestead," "You Can Farm," and "The Year Round Vegetable Gardener," and the most recent copies of MOTHER EARTH NEWS. I also enrolled in a course on organic gardening and took an online permaculture course with Geoff Lawton.

But there was a problem. At this point in time we were building what we called "our forever house," a completely round, super insulated home. It was beautiful. And expensive. Five years into the project and we still weren't finished. We were also slowly realizing we couldn't afford our dream home as the mortgage kept growing in size.

So, of course, I thought this would be the perfect time to suggest to my husband that we move. I wanted to live in a place we could actually afford and where we would have the space to raise livestock and plant a large garden.

I have to admit it took some convincing on my part to persuade my husband to abandon our five-year building project in favour of buying an old farmhouse and some cheap land. But we did the unthinkable. We put our half finished, mortgaged house up for sale and started scouring the local real estate ads for something in our price range.

We spent months searching until I stumbled upon a too-good-to-be-true listing of a farm literally footsteps from the edge of town. Being close to the city's limits was one of our criteria, you see. We didn't want to be too far from our imaginary customers, local farmers market, or the kids' school.

Since we already had a mortgage to pay on our current house, we couldn't buy the property outright. Instead we struck a rent-to-own deal for a year, and a month later we packed up our stuff and moved in.

I was so excited to begin homesteading. Only we didn't. We were spending all our time just getting the farmhouse into a livable state. The roof leaked, the electrical was outdated, and when you turned on the tap in the upstairs bathroom, water leaked from the ceiling into the downstairs kitchen.

So my days were filled with looking after the kids, and the evenings and weekends were filled with farmhouse and barn renovations.

Frustrated with our situation, I decided on a whim that I would start a blog (theoldwalshfarm.com) describing our journey to date and what we hoped to accomplish. And suddenly I knew what to do.

Thinking about, and writing down, our dreams in that first post reminded me that we needed a plan. The kind of plan I would have been asked to make in business class at university. I could picture my professor saying, "People don't plan to fail. Instead they fail to plan."

So I dreamed. I even made one of those corny dream boards. I thought about what I really saw myself doing and I made a list of things I wanted to accomplish, when I wanted to do them, and what resources I'd need to make them happen. And then I came up with an idea. We would set out to learn 52 homesteading skills in one year.

Now I have confession. I really like making plans. I really, really, really, really like making plans. I'm one of those people who secretly takes pleasure in making lists and buys waaaaaay too many notepads and calendars. But I can't say I always follow these wonderful plans I make. I try. I really do. But it doesn't always happen.

This time though I couldn't afford to fail. I had banked everything on making this homesteading deal work. So when I came up with the idea of this challenge, I decided to share what I was learning on my newly established blog. I announced to every single one of my friends and family members — and everyone I knew on social media (as well as anyone else who would listen to my story) — about my goal, which wasn't that many people to tell you the truth, but it didn't matter. It was enough to hold me accountable. And guess what? September was not only the month we began our quest, it's also the month we successfully finished learning 52 homesteading skills in one year.

Now it's your turn. If you haven't already begun your homesteading adventure, what the heck are you waiting for? Raise your pitchfork, shovel, trowel, or whatever farming implement you have on hand and let's do this!

The Art of Fermentation

Water Bath Canning

Feed Your Bees

Drying Herbs

project 36

the art of fermentation

Have you seen them? They're easy to spot. The enterprising individuals who prepare dozens of jars of tomatoes and strawberry jam and then proudly post their freshly canned goods on Facebook. You've probably seen them at the farmers market, arms full of baskets of cucumbers, smug in the satisfaction that if the world's food supply ends, they won't go hungry. Oh no! They will have pickles.

For years I've thought, "I should do that too." But somehow I'd end up convincing myself I didn't have the time, energy or expertise. Well, not this year. This is the year I become a real homesteader, darn it. And I did. This month. And I can't believe I haven't fermented pickles before. It's actually so easy my kids can do it.

Note to self: Next year get the kids to do all my canning work. Although, we will really have to work on not eating the produce. Sigh.

So do you want to know how easy it is? It's so simple that all you really need to make fermented pickles is water, salt, and cucumbers. If you want to get fancy, you can add spices.

You put this stuff in jars and then you observe. That's right. It ferments all by itself. All you need to do is stand back and watch as your plain old cucumbers turn into delightful, crunchy pickles that are now more healthy than the original cucumbers.

What is fermentation and why should I eat it?

Fermentation is the ancient art of pickling, a technique used long before there was canning. Fermenting turns your food into natural probiotics. So instead of popping a probiotic pill, you can eat fermented foods, which, according to Dr. Joseph Mercola, actually contain 100 times more probiotics than a pricey supplement.

One quick Google search on the internet will result in tonnes of information on the health benefits of probiotics, from boosting your immune system to detoxifying your body. I don't know if it's all true, but I think I feel better after I eat a fermented pickle, don't you?

Forget about investing in the stock market — make pickles.

Now before I get into the details of pickle making, I have a secret to share. I regularly go to a local health foods store and buy jars of fermented pickles that must have real gold dust in them since each jar costs about $9.99.

Now my husband has no idea how much these pickles cost so to any family members out there who I know will read every word of my book (right, guys?), don't mention it, OK? Anyway, the point is you can grow your own cucumbers for the price of seeds, and a little hard work. And since water is free and salt is cheap, the cost savings of making your own is huge. Forget about investing in the stock market — start making pickles!

Crunchy Fermented Pickles

ingredients & supplies

- pickling jars: I used 1 L sized mason jars
- pickling salt
- un-chlorinated water (let your water stand overnight and the chlorine will evaporate)
- cucumbers: I'm told it's best, especially if you want crunchy pickles, to choose the small pickling cucumbers
- grape or oak leaves, if you can find them
- spices of your choice: dill, parsley or lemon balm, mustard seeds, hot chilies, onion, garlic cloves, etc.

instructions

- Wash and dry your mason jars.

- Dissolve your salt in a pot of water. I wanted a really salty, sour pickle so I used 2½ tbsp of salt for each 1 L jar.

- Wash your cucumbers and put aside any bruised or questionable looking cucumbers. Freshness is one of the keys to crunchy pickles so if in doubt, try soaking them in iced water for a couple hours.

- Cut the ends off the cucumbers. Actually, you really only need to slice the flower ends off the cucumbers as they contain enzymes that can soften the pickles during fermentation. But I wasn't taking any chances. I just cut both ends off. You can also pierce the cucumbers with a fork a few times to allow the brine to better penetrate.

- I added either a grape or oak leaf, which supposedly maintains the crispiness of the pickles thanks to their natural tannins. I put one leaf on the bottom of each jar along with my spices. I tried all kinds of combinations: dill and garlic; bay leaves and onions; cinnamon and cloves; lemon balm and lovage (a perennial herb that tastes like celery).

- Pack your cucumbers tightly into the jar and cover with brine, leaving about 1 inch of headspace so your bottles don't explode when the brine begins to ferment. Now this is really important: The brine should cover the vegetables at all times or else they will start developing mould and your pickles will be ruined. As long as they remain under the anaerobic safety of the brine, they should be fine.
Note: To prevent any little pieces of herbs or spices from floating to the surface, I used whole pieces of herbs and wrapped any smaller spices, such as cloves and peppercorns, in a grape leaf and stuffed them in the bottom of my jar. This is only necessary if you not using something such as a fermentation weight to keep your vegetables submerged.

- Screw on the lids (but not too tightly; you want to let some of the fermentation gasses escape) and set in a location at room temperature, out of direct sunlight. Soon you'll see bubbles of carbon dioxide gas in the brine, which means you've been successful and the brine has started to acidify.

- Now here is the tricky part. There doesn't seem to be a cut and dry date as to when fermented pickles are done. It depends on the temperature of your home and how sour you like your pickles. On average, full sour pickles usually ferment at a cool room temperature for six days.

- Once the pickles are done to your liking, screw the lids on tight and store in the fridge or cold storage to slow further fermentation. Your pickles should keep for a year or even longer.

Now, you too, can proudly post your freshly canned produce on Facebook and take comfort in the fact that you have jars and jars of pickles stashed away to get you through the winter. Unfortunately, I can't say the same about the peach slices I tried to can this month. Total failure. Unless you like soggy, floating peaches. But I called it a "delicious disaster" because it led to ...

project 37

water bath canning

I was not supposed to make pumpkin spiced peach sauce. I was going to can dozens and dozens of sliced peaches and show everyone how fun it could be.

But it was a disaster. I ended up with four jars of peaches. Four. Oh, we'll definitely make it through the winter now. If there's an emergency, you can all come over and share my four jars of soggy, floating peaches. Yes, it's true. My canned peaches were pitiful. They turned mushy (boiling them before packing was a mistake) and because I didn't pack them tight enough in the jar, the result was floating fruit. But I'd like to point out (to make myself feel better), the peaches are still safe to eat and, in fact, tasty, according to our official taste tester. "Wow!" exclaimed my daughter. "They taste just like peaches. Mommy, you're a professional." I love that girl! The good news is I tried again and discovered something even better than canned sliced peaches ...

Trust me. After you try pumpkin spiced peach sauce, you'll wonder why you wanted to can sliced peaches in the first place. I am now dreaming of slathering this stuff over pancakes, cakes, yogurt, ice cream or just plain eating it straight out of the jar.

Pumpkin Spice Peach Sauce

ingredients

- yellow peaches (not white peaches)
- pumpkin spice (use one teaspoon of pumpkin spice per 4 cups of peach purée)
- lemon juice (1 tsp per jar)

equipment

Before we get started, I must admit that when I first looked into water bath canning, I was completely overwhelmed. It seemed like you needed a special degree in canning or you'd die of botulism. Just the list of equipment was enough to intimidate me. So I bought a canning kit that included a 21-quart canner, jar lifter, lid lifter, funnel, bubble remover, and other knick-knacks.

Now that I've actually tried canning, I realize I could have done without everything except the jar lifter, which I ended up breaking. Some people might make the mistake of using the plastic end instead of the rubber end and guess what? The plastic will break in the hot water. Yeah, I know. I may not be the smartest homesteader on the block.

So what equipment do you really need? A large canning pot with a metal rack to hold the jars off the bottom of the pot where they could break due to the extra heat, mason jars, and something to lift the hot jars out of the scalding water. You don't need a special tool to remove bubbles (a simple spatula will do) and a funnel is nice, but if you're handy with a spoon, it's not necessary.

Now that we've got the equipment out of the way, let's get started. Although the list of steps may seem complicated, it really isn't. You do have to be able to follow instructions, but other than that, it's actually quite simple.

pumpkin spice recipe

1 tsp cinnamon

2 tsp ground ginger

1 tsp nutmeg

½ tsp ground allspice

½ tsp ground cloves

instructions

1. Wait until your peaches are ripe and then toss them in the freezer. I only meant to leave mine in the freezer for a couple hours, but they ended up sitting there overnight. No harm done. Note: You will need about 2 to 3 pounds of peaches per quart jar (about 4 to 6 medium peaches).

2. Wash your jars and lids in hot soapy water. In the past, it was also recommended to sterilize the jars and lids, but if your water bath processing time will be over 10 minutes, which it is for peach sauce, this step is no longer necessary. Your jars do need to be warm so as not to risk breakage when you add the jar to a hot canner. So make sure you wash them in hot water.

3. Run your peaches under lukewarm water and like magic the peels will slip off. I was skeptical of this little peeling tip, but it really works.

4. Make a peach sculpture. OK, this isn't necessary, but it's a lot of fun.

5. Once the peaches have thawed enough to cut through, chop your peaches into quarters and toss the pits.

6. Place the peaches in a saucepan, bring to a boil and let simmer for 2 to 5 minutes. This is called "hot-packing." It helps keep the food from floating in the jars, increases the vacuum seal, and improves shelf life.

7. Add 1 tsp of pumpkin spice per four cups of purée. Purée the peaches in a blender until smooth.

8. Spoon the peach sauce into your jars to within ½ inch of the top rim and add 1 tsp of lemon juice to each jar to help preserve the colour.

9. Remove air bubbles by running a spatula around the inside of the jar.

10. Wipe jar rims clean to ensure a proper seal.

11. Add the lid and rings and screw them on "fingertip" tight. If the lids are put on too tightly, any air bubbles that weren't removed in Step 9 can't escape during the hot water bath canning process and your lids could buckle.

12. Place the jars into your canning pot on top of the rack. Fill your pot with water, ensuring there is at least 1 inch of water above the tops of the lids.

13. Once the rolling boil has settled, use a jar lifter to remove the jars and set them aside to cool for 24 hours. After cooling, check your seals. The lids shouldn't move when you push down with your finger and if you remove the rings, you should be able to lift the jar into the air by the lid alone.

Label and store your jars in a cool, dark place for up to a year.

And that's it. Canning is definitely a homesteading art form that may take a little practice. But watch out! It's addictive. Soon, you'll be bringing home dozens of canning recipe books from the library and packing up everything from tomatoes to fiddleheads and gifting them to all your lucky friends. I'm sure they will be very grateful to receive a jar of fiddleheads for Christmas instead of the gift you normally buy them. Am I right?

Here are the guidelines if you live below 1,000 feet elevation:
500 ml — 20 minutes
1 litre — 25 minutes
1.5 litre — 35 minutes
If you live above 1,000 feet elevation, you'll have to process your canned goods longer.
For example:
1,001 to 3,000 feet — add 5 minutes
3,001 to 6,000 feet — add 10 minutes
6,001 to 8,000 feet — add 15 minutes

project 38
feeding your bees

I gave my bees diarrhea. How did this happen? Well, I had hoped I wouldn't have to feed my bees. I thought they could thrive solely on their own honey. But one summer of beekeeping taught me otherwise. Bees may not be our pets, but we are their keepers and it is our job to look out for them when hard times hit.

So when the nectar stopped flowing and my bees needed food, I didn't hesitate to go to the store and buy raw, organic sugar. Why raw organic? I love my bees and I didn't want them to ingest any pesticides. And they didn't. Instead they got diarrhea (honeybee dysentery). Whoops! Turns out some of the extra nutrients in organic sugar do not agree with bees. Plain, white granulated sugar is the best option.

So although feeding your bees may sound so easy it shouldn't even be a skill, there is a correct and incorrect way to do this. There's also a when, if, should you, how much, and what kind. Basically, it's complicated and I'm not sure there is really one "right" way. But here are a couple reasons why you may have to feed your bees and how I feed mine:

There's an early heavy frost
The best food for bees is obviously honey but sometimes colonies use up their winter stores before the nectar starts flowing again in the fall. This could be because of an early heavy frost. Without any flowers, there is no nectar for the bees to collect yet there is still brood to be fed. As these new bees emerge, they will leave behind empty cells that should be filled with honey. In this scenario, it would be wise to provide your bees with syrup so they can fill those empty cells and have enough stores to make it through the long, cold winter.

It is your first year of beekeeping
Normally, in my cold climate, you should overwinter your bees with a bottom brood box (I use a medium) as well as two additional medium boxes full of honey. But despite their best efforts (and without harvesting any honey), my new colony was only able to fill the brood box and one other medium. In this case, I had no choice but to feed my bees in the fall or they would have starved.

There's a nectar dearth
A nectar dearth is a shortage of nectar-producing flowers usually caused by the heat and a lack of rain. I would have never known what a nectar dearth was if it wasn't for my beekeeping mentor, George, who warned me to feed my bees. In fact, at the time, I didn't even have a pail to feed them with and had to borrow one from him. Lesson learned!

What should I feed my bees?

If the temperature is at least 10°C

Feed your bees sugar syrup. Depending on the season, there are different recipes. Spring syrup is light like the nectar bees collect from flowers. In the Fall, syrup is heavy like honey to help the bees boost their winter stores. It's also thick enough that it won't freeze. It is estimated that one gallon of heavy syrup will increase colony reserves by about seven pounds.

Below are the simple recipes to make your own syrup. Although it's not necessary, I also add a couple drops of Honey-B-Healthy or Pro Health to my syrup. The essential oils such as spearmint and lemongrass are supposed to improve the health of your hive.

spring sugar syrup

- one part water
- one part plain white granulated sugar
- Honey-B-Healthy (optional), follow package directions

fall sugar syrup

- one part water
- two parts plain white granulated sugar
- Honey-B-Healthy (optional), follow package directions

directions

Heat the water and mix in the sugar until it is completely dissolved. Allow to cool to room temperature before using.

I pour the sugar syrup into what's called a pail feeder. It is simply a container with a lid that you invert over the hole in your inner cover. There is a smaller hole covered in mesh in the lid that allows the bees to remove the syrup. The syrup does not drip down into the hive thanks to Boyle's Law — you remember that from high school science class, right?

Once the pail is full of syrup, you tip it upside down. A few drops will slip out until the pressure equalizes. Then simply set the pail on top of your inner cover.

I cover the pail with an empty super and the hive roof to prevent any other bees or insects from trying to rob my hive of its syrup.

If you don't want to spend the money on a special pail, you could try using a Mason jar with a few holes poked in the metal lid.

If the temperature is below 10°C

At this temperature the bees cluster together to stay warm. They will not leave their cluster to search for food. However, you may still want to leave something in the hive for them to eat in case of an emergency. Pail feeding with syrup may not be a good choice because temperature changes (freeze/thaw/freeze) may cause the pail to expand and contract causing syrup to leak onto the bees chilling them and perhaps even killing them.

But you can leave fondant or make your own candy board. During the winter, when there is a brief thaw and temperatures rise, the bees can break cluster and search out the food.

Although honey is the best food for bees, don't be afraid to feed your colony in emergency situations. It is better to feed them sugar then let them die.

project 39

drying herbs

The nursery plant tag read: "Easy to grow." What it should have read was: "This is a weed."

I have now learned to be skeptical of any plants that are "easy to grow" because what this usually means is that they spread uncontrollably. Of course, I didn't know this when I first started my perennial herb garden earlier this summer. What was supposed to be an attractively arranged herb garden mixed with vegetables and flowers turned into a jungle where only the fittest survive.

Who is responsible? Two big garden bullies named chamomile and lemon balm who are overtaking everything else in their vicinity. Both herbs should come with this warning: Plant only in locations where nothing else will survive.

This month I showed them who is boss. It was time to dry herbs. I think this is my favourite homesteading skill so far. My husband says it's because I don't have to do anything, but the real reason is because of the smell. Our house is now filled with the sweet and spicy scents of chamomile, lemon balm, and lavender. They also happen to make the perfect cup of soothing, homemade tea, but more on that later.

I harvested my herbs in the morning after the dew had dried and before it started to get hot. Normally, it's not recommended to harvest more than 75 percent of one plant at a time, but I wasn't worried about this when it came time to cut the lemon balm. I'm pretty sure it will survive.

So I cut huge swaths of it, wrapped them in twine and hung them in my bathroom until they turned dry and crispy. Yes, the bathroom. It's a tiny room with a dehumidifier, which means things dry fast. I will admit there is one drawback to this method. You can't shower. But that's OK. My family was happy to hose off outside for a couple days. Well, the kids were, my husband not so much.

Anyway, if this doesn't sound like your cup of tea, you can also hang your herbs in any dry location in your home out of direct sunlight — but it will take longer.

You can also speed up the process by placing them in the oven. This is a great way to dry herbs such as chamomile. Simply preheat your oven to 170 degrees. Arrange your herbs on a baking sheet and bake for 20 minutes. Then turn the oven off and leave them there overnight. Crumble and store until you're ready to steep.

By the way, did you know chamomile tea is made with the flowers? Those teeny, tiny white daisy-like flowers? If I had known this fact earlier, I might have thought twice about buying a chamomile plant because, of course, you have to pick those flowers by hand. So I cheated and added some leaves too. They aren't as strong tasting as the flowers, but still give off a nice flavour.

Despite the extra work of harvesting the chamomile, it was worth it. Chamomile, or the nighttime tea as it is often called, promotes a good night's sleep. And who can't use more of that?

In fact, the only thing better than chamomile tea to help you relax after a long week is chamomile mixed with calming lavender and lemon balm. Lemon balm is a stress reducer and may even boost your mood thanks to its ability to soothe the nervous system. So the next time you're feeling stressed out and sleepless, brew up a cup of this calming, herbal, homemade tea.

ingredients

- 1 part chamomile
- 1 part lavender
- 2 parts lemon balm
- 1 tsp honey per cup (optional)

Mix the herbs together and add a heaping teaspoon to your tea brewing cup, infuser, or good old-fashioned strainer. Cover with boiling water and steep the herbs in your favourite cup for about 10 to 15 minutes.

Enjoy before drifting off to eight hours of solid slumber with no interruptions from little sleep robbing hooligans. Yeah, you're right — the tea doesn't work that well. Save this fantasy for your dreams.

OCTOBER

Sometimes you have to think outside the box if you want to make your homesteading lifestyle work. And boy, oh, boy, was my husband surprised with my creativity when he came home to find this …

Yes, folks. I started a little grow-op in my bedroom, one of the only areas big enough to place the five-tier metal shelving unit I "borrowed" from my husband's garage. But don't worry. It's all legal and Jérémie was only slightly annoyed by the new use of his shelf. I was growing microgreens … well, until I forgot to water them. Then I was just busy crying over my lifeless seedlings and wondering who came up with the stupid idea of trying to learn 52 homesteading skills in a year.

The first month of the challenge I was feeling motivated and enthusiastic. But by the end of the second month my fiery glow had already worn off and I was questioning my ability to make it to the end. I was feeling intimidated by all the skills I still needed to learn. And, if I couldn't even can sliced peaches or keep my microgreens alive, how the heck did I think I was going to raise ducks or bees? But if I gave up and sat around the house sulking, I definitely wouldn't get anywhere. So instead of dwelling on the fact that I still had ALL these skills to learn, I forgot about the challenge and focused on each small daily or weekly task.

So this month, in addition to growing microgreens (after being more careful to regularly water them the second time around), we learned how to dry fruit and discovered a new favourite snack food — dried apple slices. We also uncovered what must be the world's easiest yogurt recipe, which uses nothing but a jar, a spoon, some milk, and yogurt starter. No heating, no cooling, and no fancy equipment required. And finally, Tiffany Thorne of Thornehill Farms in Allison, New Brunswick, was kind enough to offer to show me how to milk a goat. Now why would I want to do this when we didn't yet own one?

We were considering purchasing a goat, but didn't feel knowledgeable enough to just go out and get one. So as part of our challenge we planned to learn some of the basic skills related to dairy animals before we brought one home to the farm. This was one of the few wise decisions we made. After just one lesson, I realized milking a goat is a lot harder than it looks. And, as Tiffany pointed out to me, dairy animals are also a huge commitment, requiring you to routinely milk them once or twice a day for at least half of the year — even if you are sick with the stomach flu.

Now I'm not saying we will never have a dairy animal because I still have high hopes for one in the future. We had a lot of fun making yogurt, butter, and cheese. But I think it was a good idea not to jump into this in our first year. This kind of insight is one of the reasons I'm glad we took the time to sit down and make a plan and list out the skills we wanted to learn, when we wanted to do them, and what resources we'd need to make them happen.

If we hadn't, we might have overwhelmed ourselves with too many homesteading projects at once. By writing them all down and organizing them by season, and then month, and then week, we could see what would be manageable. And by spreading skills throughout the year, we could accomplish more without taking on too much. (Stop laughing. OK. OK. Maybe we were a little overwhelmed and maybe 52 skills was a bit ambitious. You might want to start with a slightly smaller, more realistic goal.)

Of course, this doesn't mean our first year homesteading was easy and nothing went wrong. As you know by now, difficulty is a common theme that runs throughout this book. I go out and try new things thinking "how hard can it be" and half the time I'm right, but the rest of the time I end up making one mistake after another.

The important thing is that you don't give up. If there is one lesson I have learned from this challenge, it's that with enough practice, you can learn ANYTHING. Maybe you won't be the fastest goat milker or scythe user in the land. Maybe you won't be an artisan cheesemaker sought out by the best restaurants in town, but you can learn to milk a goat, use a scythe, and make cheese. Yes, you can! And each skill that you learn will convince you of this too. Eventually, month after month, all these little successes will add up and give you the confidence to fulfill every one of your homesteading dreams — or at least 52 of them.

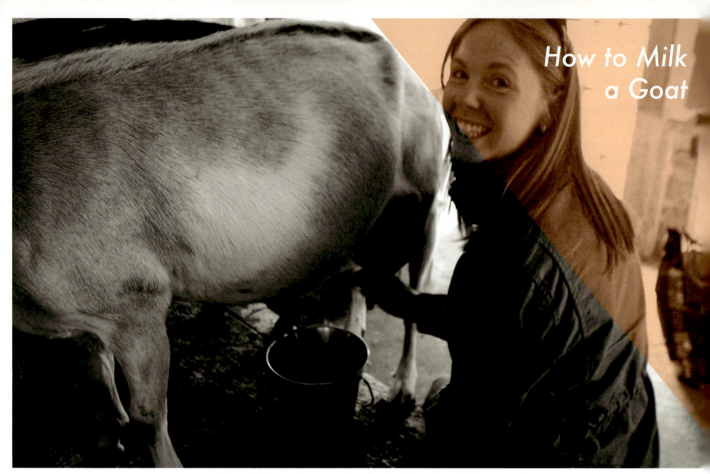

How to Milk a Goat

Dried Sweet Apple Rings

Homemade Yogurt

Starting a Grow-op

Save Your Seeds

project 40

how to milk a goat

This is so much fun. No, really! You *need* to try milking a goat. In just 20 minutes, you could walk away with a stainless steel pail full of the freshest, sweetest, and most delicious raw milk you've every tasted.

But not your first time. No. Your first experience milking a goat won't be so easy. Mine was rather embarrassing for everyone involved — me, the Alpine goat, and her owner, Tiffany Thorne.

I really wished I didn't have an audience as I desperately tried to get more than a teaspoon of milk from the poor goat. Tiffany looked on with concern while the goat, even less impressed with my skills, occasionally turned her head away from her bucket of feed to give me a VERY dirty look.

In reality, I think it might take me about five hours to milk one goat. Don't laugh. Because your first experience will likely will be the same. You know why? There is an art to this skill and it really does take practice.

However, women who've breastfed have one advantage. We have a better idea of how this is supposed to work. Nevertheless it didn't help me. I breastfed, and pumped, and still struggled. But like I told Jérémie, I'm sure I'll get better at milking with practice, right?

I don't think he is as convinced of this or of the fact that we need to have goats on our farm. But we really do because after I tasted a glass of fresh-from-the-goat milk, there is no going back. And just think of the delicious goat cheese you could make. Gee. I really need to go out and get a goat TODAY.

Tiffany, who has been raising goats since her teenage years, recommends starting with a goat who has already been milked versus a kid. Hey, at least one of you should know what you're doing, right?

She also suggests purchasing a full sized breed such as a Nubian, Alpine, Saanen, or LaMancha versus the smaller Nigerian Dwarfs. They are cute and they will provide you with delicious milk — but only a third of the amount of a regular-sized breed. If you are going to go to the trouble of milking a goat, why not get as much milk as you can?

directions

1. Set up a milking area. Goats are usually milked on a stand (stanchion) so you don't have to hunch over and hurt your back. Your stanchion should have a head gate to secure your goat.

2. Gather your herd. Tiffany's goats came running for their turn to get milked and hopped right onto the stand without any encouragement. Why? They couldn't wait to be relieved of their milk.

3. Provide a bucket of feed. Tiffany gives her goats Milk Generator to encourage more production and good behaviour at the milking stand since they enjoy the nutritious snack. Close their head gate on the stanchion.

4. Clean the udder using an udder wash solution.

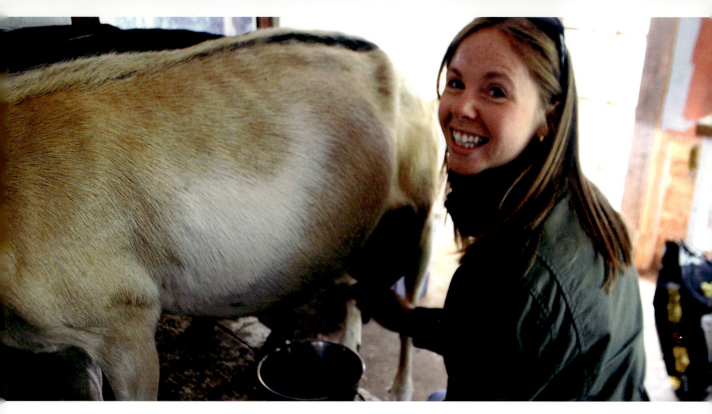

5. Using your thumb and index finger, occlude (gently close off) the teat where it meets the udder. This traps the milk in the teat so it can't flow back up into the udder. Do not let go. You need to hold on tight and then use your palm and remaining fingers to squeeze the milk out. Start with your middle, then ring and finally your pinkie finger, pushing the milk down the teat and into your pail. Then let go so the teat can fill back up with milk. Repeat.
Remember: Tugging will not get you anywhere. Occlude and squeeze. Occlude and squeeze. Occlude and squeeze. Until no more milk remains.

6. Massage or "bump" the udder like a baby goat might do to its mama. This will cause your goat to let down more milk.

7. When you're done, the udder should look wrinkled and/or shriveled and, of course, there won't be any milk left. I would like to say a big thank you to Tiffany for watching very patiently as I slowly and very badly milked her goats. She assures me that with practice, I, and anyone else who wants to take on the challenge, will get better and faster with time. And that's all I'm going to write on this subject because I have to go and buy myself a goat.

NOTE

Tiffany feeds the first few squirts of milk to her livestock guardian dogs who are just as eager as the goats come milking time. Why? The milk not only has a stronger goat flavour, but it may contain a higher amount of bacteria.

project 41

dried sweet apple rings

Please tell me I'm not the only one …. Have you ever excitedly gone to the store and bought yourself a shiny new kitchen gadget and then NEVER used it? That's the story of my dehydrator. I purchased it several years ago with the idea that I was going to save money by drying my own fruit and vegetables. It never happened.

Sometimes trying new things just feels like too much effort. You're not really sure if it is going to work or how much time will be involved. But this is one project I really shouldn't have shelved into the back of my kitchen cupboards. This has to be the easiest homesteading skill of all — the ancient art of drying food.

So this month I dusted off my dehydrator and even found the accompanying instructions. Well, kind of. A big hole was torn in the middle of where it actually tells you how to use the machine. Thankfully, there's nothing complicated about drying apples. As an added bonus, you'll also avoid the sulphites and sugar often found in pricey store-bought versions of dried fruits.

directions

1. Use an apple peeler to core, cut, and remove the peel from your apples. You can purchase one for less than $15. If you don't have one, it is totally worth the few bucks.

2. Dip each apple slice into lemon water (⅛ cup of lemon juice mixed into 2 cups of water) to prevent the apples from browning.

3. Arrange the apple slices evenly on the drying trays. The apple slices will shrink so they can be touching slightly. Sprinkle the apple slices with your favourite seasoning. Turn them over and sprinkle again. I used a mix of 1 tsp cinnamon, ¼ tsp nutmeg, ¼ tsp allspice, and a pinch of cloves.

4. Plug in your machine and enjoy the delicious baked apple aroma. Approximately 24 hours later you will have a sweet and crispy treat that will last in your cupboard for many years. But that won't happen. I had to risk my life protecting these apple rings from my hungry family so I could get a picture of them for you.

To be honest, I was trying to make soft and chewy apple rings, but I left them in the dehydrator too long. If you think you'd prefer a more raisin-like consistency, your apple rings may be ready in about 12 hours. The exact amount of time will vary depending on the type of apple you use and the thickness of your slices.

Store your rings in airtight containers in a dark hiding spot so little, and maybe even big, hands can't easily find them.

project 42

easy homemade yogurt

Yeah, right, Kimberlee. Homemade yogurt so easy your 3-year-old can make it? I don't believe you. Oh yes, he can! Because I've scoured the globe to find the easiest — and I mean the very, very easiest — way to make homemade yogurt. Are you ready for this?

1. You pour milk in a jar and add some starter yogurt.
2. You let the milk sit on your counter until it turns to yogurt.

The end. That's it! Really, that's all it takes to make yogurt. And you can save upwards of $700 a year by making your own. If you've never made yogurt, maybe you're not that impressed. But the traditional way of making yogurt involves heating your milk, stirring your milk, cooling your milk … Basically, you need time and patience. If not, you end up with milk, not yogurt. Just trust me on this one.

I never had enough time or patience — until now. Now I'm back in the yogurt making business thanks to a little known yogurt starter called Filmjölk from Canadian culture experts — Culture Mother (www.culturemother.ca). They sell several varieties of yogurt cultures, which can all be used at room temperature. If you like the taste and texture of commercial yogurts, you'll want to try Vili, a mild tasting yogurt with a smooth texture. But, much to my family's dismay, I decided to try Filmjölk, a thick, custard-like yogurt with a cheesy flavour. Because who doesn't like cheesy yogurt? What? You don't?

OK, I'll be honest. I'm the only one in our family who likes it. I've been using it as a vegetable dip and enjoying the occasional bowlful for breakfast topped with cinnamon and oranges. But I understand not everyone likes cottage cheese-like yogurt. In that case, go for the Vili or check out another of the yogurt starter options from Culture Mother.

The point is if your family enjoys yogurt and you have literally two seconds a week to spare, you could not only save yourself upwards of $700 a year by making your own, but you'll also be on your way to becoming a really cool homesteader like me. Oh, come on! I'm cool, or rad, or whatever the kids are saying these days. Hmm … maybe no one cool ever said rad. Yeah, OK. So I might be more of a homesteading geek. But never mind that. Make the yogurt. Save yourself some money and do yourself proud. But first …

how much you'll save

- Cost of yogurt: Approx. $1.60 to $2.33 per cup
- Cost of milk: $0.44 per cup
- Cost of cereal cream: $0.82 per cup
- SAVINGS: $0.78 to $1.89 per cup

Our family of four goes through approximately two litres of yogurt a week. By making our own, we can save $6.24 to $15.12 a week. Over a year, that's $324.48 to $786.24. Think of what you could do with that money. You could save up for a cow or a goat! What are you waiting for? Let's start making homemade yogurt.

ingredients

- Milk, cream, coconut milk, soy, almond milk
- Yogurt starter

> **NOTE**
> To activate your yogurt starter, you will need to use pure cow's or goat's milk. After that, you can use any alternative milk. If it doesn't thicken enough to your liking, you can strain it.

directions

1. Follow the directions that come with your yogurt starter to activate your culture.

2. Pour your milk or cream into a jar and stir in 1 tbsp of yogurt starter for every cup of milk/cream. (The instructions for Filmjölk recommends cream over milk for a thick, Greek-style yogurt. Otherwise, use milk.)

3. Cover with a cloth and let sit at room temperature until your yogurt has the consistency of custard, approximately 12 to 48 hours. It may take longer if your room temperature is cooler than 20°C.

4. Screw on a tight-fitting lid and refrigerate until ready to serve. I still can't believe this works. It is one of those things that just seems too easy to be true. But for once, it really is this easy. And as long as you save a small portion of your pure, unflavoured yogurt to make the next batch, you can continue making homemade yogurt forever. Aren't you excited?

project 43

starting a grow-op

How do you feel about growing vegetables in your bedroom? I agree. It's not the ideal location, but this was the only space big enough for my grand microgreen growing setup. I had visions of producing hundreds of pounds of food year round with little effort.

Why microgreens? Previously, I had tried growing sprouts — those tiny shoots grown without soil. Within days you can produce your own salad. But even though I grew all kinds of beautiful looking sprouts, they weren't as tasty as I had hoped.

Now I don't want to turn anyone off of growing sprouts because I have friends who love them. But my sprouts tasted a lot like their growing medium — water.

So this year I decided to try something different. Microgreens! These flavour bombshells grow almost as fast as sprouts, but in soil. And they are sweeter and tastier — in my humble opinion — than anything you can find at the supermarket. They're also a whole lot less expensive. For example, a $5.49 bag of alfalfa seeds can produce up to 40 cups of nutritious sprouts. And when I say nutritious, I mean you can stop taking your multivitamin. A University of Maryland study found that microgreens have up to 40 times more concentrated nutrients than their mature counterparts. But I am not going to tell you just how easy they were to grow because not all of mine survived my first attempt.

fun facts

- An angry 3-year-old can stomp on your baby seedlings and they will survive.

- A soccer ball can land on your microgreens and they will live.

- You can put a bag over your head and pretend you are a robot and accidentally knock your microgreens over and they will still be salvageable.

- You can forget your microgreens on the floor in very low lighting and they will grow — tall and stringy — but they won't die.

- You can forget to water your microgreens for days and they will ... they will perish. Oh yes, they will.

But it wasn't just the watering that proved to be a challenge. It was getting the grow-op started. There is a lot of stuff you need to gather before you can start growing.

I will admit that once you are fully equipped, the microgreens pretty much grow themselves as long as you are handy with a watering can/spray bottle. You might want to set up some watering reminders.

ingredients

- A place to grow your microgreens. You probably don't need a five-tier metal shop shelf in your bedroom (although I like to think it adds a special ambiance to the room). It does help to find a place with either enough south facing sun (about six hours of bright light) or where grow lights can be installed.

- Growing containers, preferably with drainage. I went with the standard black trays, but you can have fun with this and grow in something funky like a teapot or a decorative bowl.

- Potting soil, worm castings, liquid seaweed.

- Seeds: I love Mumm's non-GMO, organic sprouting seeds (sprouting.com). Although the seeds are not all grown on the family farm in Saskatchewan, Canada (not everything can be grown in our Canadian climate), they are all from certified organic farms. Try their Ancient Eastern salad mix made up of fenugreek, lentils, kamut, and adzuki beans, or a mix of curly cress, alfalfa, peas, corn, and sunflower shoots. Put them together with a few homegrown mesclun mix salad greens and you've got one awesome salad.

If you are using artificial lights, you don't have to purchase special grow lights, which can cost hundreds of dollars. We simply use an LED 4,000 K shop light.

HELPFUL TIP: You will need to plug your light into a three-pronged plug. After lugging our metal shelf upstairs and getting everything set up, I realized all of our plugs are two pronged. This is kind of like when we discovered (shortly after purchasing our house) there is no heat in the upstairs of our home.

directions

1. Spread your potting soil to a depth of about two to three inches and add a thin layer of worm castings. I also like to fortify my soil with liquid seaweed.

2. Except for large seeds like sunflowers and pea sprouts, sow your microgreen seeds densely. I plant the larger seeds in the soil and sprinkle the smaller ones on top.

3. Thoroughly wet the whole area with a spray bottle. Be careful not to overdo it. You don't want the seeds to be sitting in water.

4. Cover with a second tray or plastic bag to trap moisture.

5. As soon as you can see the first sprout, remove your cover.

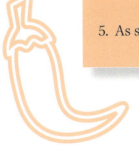

when to harvest?

You can harvest when the first two leaves open or wait and harvest as needed. Your seed package will tell you approximately when the microgreens should be ready. For example, cress can be harvested in just a few days after sowing whereas sunflower seeds can take up to 12 days.

And that's it! From now on you will no longer bring home those sad salad greens that have been shipped hundreds of miles from their growing location. Instead you will enjoy an endless supply of gorgeously fresh and nutritious microgreen salads grown right in your bedroom. Imagine getting up in the morning and plucking a healthy breakfast from your side table? You are totally going to do this. Right?

project 44

saving your seeds

Do you believe in signs? I think I do. Let me take you back in time. I grew up as your typical city slicker. But my heart ... it belonged in the country with my grandma. Every summer I would travel to the beautiful and very rural beach town of Malagash, Nova Scotia. It was there in my grandma's garden that I first dug potatoes, picked peas, and planted worms (back then I wasn't as picky about what I grew).

Unfortunately, I didn't realize the incredible opportunity I had to learn from my grandma who was truly a master gardener. She not only grew up on a farm and lived on whatever her family could grow through the Great Depression and in post-war Denmark, but after immigrating to Canada, she started her own 500-acre farm. Sometimes, as we played cards or shelled peas at her kitchen table, she would entertain me with stories from when she was a girl. I remember her recounting tales of milking the family cow, one of her favourite farm chores despite the fact that she was often scolded afterwards for swiping the rich cream from the top of the full pail.

It was through these kinds of stories, and the delicious farm-fresh meals she would prepare, that I learned an important lesson — a gardener and her family eat better than any King or Queen. Only they get to enjoy the most delicious food right from their own backyard. So when I had children of my own, I started thinking fondly of my grandma's garden. I wanted my kids to enjoy the same fresh and nutritious food that I was so lucky to have enjoyed.

Sadly, my grandma never got to see her love of gardening take root in me. She passed away in 2012. Words cannot describe my grief or how much I miss her, but she unknowingly left me with a gift: her seeds. It must have been a sign when my mom asked if I would like to have them. I may not have been able to prevent my grandma's death, but I could keep her garden, and her traditions, alive.

I shouldn't have been surprised that my grandma saved her own seeds from year to year. In fact, she would probably think buying packages of seeds was a ridiculous waste of money when you could gather your own for free.

Now I wish I could say that I was as good as she was at saving them. But I haven't been as diligent or as successful as I would like. In fact, my husband laughed when I said I was going to write about how to save seeds since it was Jérémie who did the bulk of the saving. I was so exhausted by the end of the gardening season that buying packages of seed seemed like a perfectly rational idea.

But don't listen to me. It's truly worth the effort. Yes, you'll save money, but you'll also improve your crops each year by selecting from your best tasting, hardiest, or biggest vegetables, for example. Over time, your crops will also evolve to adapt to your local climate and growing conditions.

So here are a few seed saving tips from someone who has had mediocre success with this skill. This is exactly the type of advice you were hoping to read, right? Thankfully, my friends over at Broadfork Farm in River Hebert, Nova Scotia, are much more knowledgeable and they have provided input on all the gardening topics throughout this book.

Choose heirloom or open-pollinated seeds

Some seeds are hybrids. In seed catalogues, they often have (F1) next to the variety name. Basically, they're a cross between two different species or varieties. You can save these seeds, but they may not turn out to be exactly like their parents. If you have hybrid seed, this could be a fun experiment. Imagine! Over the years, you could create and name your own unique variety. Or you could be stuck with a funky looking, bland-tasting tomato. It's a toss-up! So, if you want to know exactly what kind of veggies you are going to eat, choose heirloom, or open-pollinated (OP) seed. An heirloom is technically an open-pollinated variety that's been in existence for at least 50 years.

Avoid cross contamination

You can save the seed from your open-pollinated and heirloom plants and expect identical seedlings as long as their pollen has not been mixed with another variety. The wind, insects, or birds, for example, can all transfer pollen from one plant to another.

Now, some veggies like beans, peas, pepper, and tomatoes are self pollinated, which means the flowers can pollinate themselves. You can reduce the chances of cross pollination by simply planting different varieties at least 10 feet apart. Seeds of Diversity Canada (www.seeds.ca) is a good resource in regards to isolation distances for different crops.

Other veggies such as cucumbers, corn, and squash are pollinated by the wind and insects. In this case, you can place a paper bag over the flower you will be harvesting seed from or place fine netting over the entire plant after first hand-pollinating them. If you don't take this precaution, you could end up with the hybrid seed situation I just described above. An easier solution might be to simply grow one variety of each species in your garden. For example, instead of planting 10 different kinds of the *Cucurbita pepo* species (this includes zucchini, most pumpkins as well as acorn, delicata, and spaghetti squash), simply plant one.

My parents once tried to save the seed from their favourite squash variety. Unfortunately, they also grew several other kinds in their garden. Unbeknownst to them, their plants were cross pollinated (most likely by the bees). When they planted the seed the next year, they were puzzled and unpleasantly surprised by this new stringy, tasteless squash in their garden.

Beware of biennials

Some storage crops such as onions, rutabagas, beets, broccoli, and cabbage are biennials. This means you will only be able to save their seed in their second year of life. So instead of harvesting these vegetables in the fall, you let them stay in the garden over winter or store them in root cellar-like conditions. In the spring, they should flower and go to seed. Sounds simple, right?

Unfortunately, we didn't have any success. Take the biennial carrot, for example. I left a couple carrots in the ground over winter in hopes of harvesting seed the following summer. But instead of growing flowers (and seeds) the following spring, my carrots rotted in the ground. FAILURE!

I didn't realize our winters may not only be too cold to overwinter these root crops, but that we get too many freeze and thaw cycles to successfully harvest seed the next year. I should have at least heavily mulched or more likely dug up the roots and stored them in soil in a root cellar or other cold storage facility that doesn't freeze.

Seed saving for beginners

I may have failed with biennials, but I had great success saving annual seed most likely because you don't have to do anything special. Take beans and peas, for example. You actually let the pods dry on the plant. You then bring them inside and bribe your kids into taking the seeds out.

Tomatoes, peppers, cucumber, squash, and melon seeds are also easy to harvest. Simply remove the seeds, rinse them, and dry them thoroughly. Most sources suggest a paper towel. We use a wooden cutting board.

Note: The seeds of tomatoes are supposed to ferment in the fruit before you can rinse and dry them. I didn't purposely do this. I just didn't get around to harvesting them right away so they sat on my counter for a few days before I harvested them. For once, being a procrastinator paid off! Saving radish and lettuce seed is also simple. In the summer, they usually "bolt," which means they grow flowers. Once the flower head matures and fully dries, you can snip the head and save the seed.

Once you've collected your seeds, it is always a good idea to let them air dry for a few weeks. Then store them in a cool, dry location. Humidity and heat are a seed's worst enemies. I keep mine in their original seed packets in a dark cupboard.

Saving seed is truly an important skill every homesteader should learn not only for themselves but for the generations who will come after them. You never know! You may be sowing a legacy for wannabe farmers in your own family who will truly appreciate these precious heirlooms that otherwise would have been lost.

NOVEMBER

I could see it in her eyes … the dreaded realization that I was going to be much more challenging than she thought.

It was my first knitting class and I spent the first 30 minutes just trying to coax yarn onto my needle. Things were getting downright embarrassing. As I looked up at my patient teacher and down at my empty knitting needles, I realized I was going to have start swallowing … pride that is.

I'm not a crafty person, so I'm not sure what made me think learning to knit was going to be easy. If I could have fled, I probably would have, but I was with my daughter. I had to set a good example and prove to her that we (well, me actually) could do this. Fortunately, expert knitter and teacher Stephanie Perry from SPerry Handmade in Moncton, New Brunswick, told me to toss the needles and lay the yarn on the table. It worked and I was able to follow her motions and "cast on" my first stitch.

After the two-hour lesson was over, I was sent home with a knitting pattern and told to do the best I could. I doubt Stephanie had high hopes, but even she must have been surprised when I came back the next week. Although I left with the beginnings of what was supposed to become a dishcloth, I showed up with nothing. Nada. How is that even possible, you ask? I messed up and had to start all over. Except I couldn't remember how. So lesson No. 2 began much like the first one with me red faced, and sweating,

and wondering what the heck I had gotten myself into. Miracles of miracles, I did eventually catch on. A few weeks later and ta da ...

OK, so I admit there are a few things wrong with this dishcloth. It's supposed to be square and I didn't quite get the pattern right in the middle, but my sweet daughter tells me it's creative. And by the way, no one is EVER going to clean anything with it. This masterpiece is going to be framed and hung so everyone can admire its lopsidedness. So what did I learn from this experience?

I'm crazy

Who wants to spend hours and hours knitting when you can just go to the store and buy the same item for a few bucks? Yes, there is likely something wrong with my brain chemistry, but there is also something alluring about learning to knit. Once you get the hang of it, it's relaxing and fun. Really! It's like yoga or mediation, but you get a new dishcloth at the end. Research describes it as an antidepressant and hey, it's a lot cheaper than therapy.

Knitting isn't just for grandmas

Knitting happens to be a very cool, hip art form. In fact, the Craft Yarn Council reports that a third of women ages 25 to 35 now knit or crochet.

Knitting eliminates boredom

What do you do when you're waiting in the doctor's office, stuck in the airport, or the most dreaded of all — waiting at the hospital? You knit. You can also knit and watch TV at the same time. So when your husband asks, "What are you doing watching Netflix reruns of *Once Upon A Time* for the FIFTH time this week?" You can say it's just on for background noise. You're actually being productive with your time. You're learning to knit.

When I wasn't trying to master this skill, I was taking out my knitting frustrations on our fruit trees. Pruning turned out to be a therapeutic experience, which may have resulted in a few too many chopped branches. Although not on our original list of 52 skills to learn, a trip to the local gardening store (a dangerous place for any homesteader) resulted in a new indoor plant — a lemon tree, which I excitedly placed upstairs in a south-facing window with dreams of large glasses of fresh lemonade. Lemons also happen to be one of the main ingredients in the cough syrup I prepared for the upcoming cold season.

As you can see, there are lots of challenging activities to tackle this winter on the homestead. So you don't ever have to just sit back, relax, and enjoy the fruits of your labour. Isn't that great? You can be productive year round! What? You think you'd like a break? Pshhhh! We still have to make candles, and butter, and get our finances in order.... Hey, stop! Wait! Get back here!

Learn to Knit

How to Prune a Fruit Tree

Indoor Lemons

Sweet Lemon Honey & Thyme Cough Syrup

project 45

learn to knit a dishcloth

Have you always wanted to learn to knit, but haven't gotten around to it? I challenge you to give it a try. You can do this. All you need is an abundance of patience, practice — and maybe a bottle of wine if it doesn't work.

This is the pattern for the dishcloth I made with the help of my mentor, Stephanie. It's a great beginner's project as you will not only practice most of the basic stitches (knit, purl, increase, decrease, cast on, and cast off), but it doesn't require a lot of knitting compared to a scarf or a hat, for example.

So what are you waiting for? Find a mentor, grab a pair of needles, find a cozy spot by the fire, and enter the exciting world of knitting. Just one warning: There is a good chance you will become obsessed with this skill. You could end up with hundreds of dollars of knitting supplies and a large closet full of yarn that you've special ordered. Knitting may lead you into learning to spin wool and thinking that buying an alpaca is a great idea. Just don't say I didn't warn you.

pattern

Cast on five stitches using a knit cast on.

increase section

K5	K2, yo, k20 (23)
K2, yo, k3 (6)	K2, yo, k5, p9, k7 (24)
K2, yo, k4 (7)	K2, yo, k22 (25)
K2 yo, k5 (8)	K2, yo, k5, p11, k7 (26)
K2, yo, k6 (9)	K2, yo, k24 (27)
K2, yo, k7 (10)	K2, yo, k5, p13, k7 (28)
K2, yo, k8 (11)	K2, yo, k26 (29)
K2, yo, k9 (12)	K2, yo, k5 p15, k7 (30)
K2, yo, k10 (13)	K2, yo, k28 (31)
K2, yo, k11 (14)	K2, yo, k5, p17, k7 (32)
K2, yo, k12 (15)	K2, yo, k30 (33)
K2, yo, k5, p1, k7 (16)	K2, yo, k5, p19, k7 (34)
K2, yo, 14 (17)	K2, yo, k32 (35)
K2, yo, k5, p3, k7 (18)	K2, yo, k5, p21, k7 (36)
K2, yo, k16 (19)	K2, yo, k34 (37)
K2, yo, k5, p5, k7 (20)	K2, yo, k5, p 23, k7 (38)
K2, yo, k18 (21)	K2, yo, k36 (39)
K2, yo, k5, p7, k7 (22)	K2, yo, k5, p25, k7 (40)

materials

- Cotton yarn (at least 40g)
- Size 4.5 mm or 5 mm needles

decrease section

K2, yo, ssk, k to last 5 sts, k2tog, k3 (39)	K2, yo, ssk, k4, p7, k3, k2tog, k3 (22)
K2, yo, ssk, k4, p 23, k3, k2tog, k3 (38)	K2, yo, ssk, k to last 5, sts, k2tog, k3 (21)
K2, yo, ssk, k to last 5 sts, k2tog, k3 (37)	K2, yo, ssk, k4, p 5 k3, k2tog, k3 (20)
K2, yo, ssk, k4, p 21, k3, k2tog, k3 (36)	K2, yo, ssk, k to last 5 sts, k2tog, k3 (19)
K2, yo, ssk, k to last 5 sts, k2tog, k3 (35)	K2, yo, ssk, k4, p3, k3, k2tog, k3 (18)
K2, yo, ssk, k4, p 19, k3, k2tog, k3 (34)	K2, yo, ssk, k to last 5 sts, k2tog, k3 (17)
K2, yo, ssk, k to last 5 sts, k2tog, k3 (33)	K2, yo, ssk, k4, p1, k3, k2tog, k3 (16)
K2, yo, ssk, k4, p 17, k3, k2tog, k3 (32)	K2, yo, ssk, k to last 5 sts, k2tog, k3 (15)
K2, yo, ssk, k to last 5 sts, k2tog, k3 (31)	K2, yo, ssk, k to last 5 sts, k2tog, k3 (14)
K2, yo, ssk, k4, p 15, k3, k2tog, k3 (30)	K2, yo, ssk, k to last 5 sts, k2tog, k3 (13)
K2, yo, ssk, k to last 5 sts, k2tog, k3 (29)	K2, yo, ssk, k to last 5 sts, k2tog, k3 (12)
K2, yo, ssk, k4, p 13, k3, k2tog, k3 (28)	K2, yo, ssk, k to last 5 sts, k2tog, k3 (11)
K2, yo, ssk, k to last 5 sts, k2tog, k3 (27)	K2, yo, ssk, k to last 5 sts, k2tog, k3 (10)
K2, yo, ssk, k4, p 11, k3, k2tog, k3 (26)	K2, yo, ssk, k to last 5 sts, k2tog, k3 (9)
K2, yo, ssk, k to last 5 sts, k2tog, k3 (25)	K2, yo, ssk, k to last 5 sts, k2tog, k3 (8)
K2, yo, ssk, k4, p 9, k3, k2tog, k3 (24)	k2 yo ssk, k2tog, k2 (7)
K2, yo, ssk, k to last 5 sts, k2tog, k3 (23)	k2, ssk, k3 (6)
	K2, k2tog, k2 (5)
	Bind off all stitches using knit bind off.

Stephanie Perry | SPerry Handmade 2016

finishing

Weave in ends and clip tails. If desired, you can block this project using a steam iron, or simply run it through the washer and dryer.

project 46

how to prune a fruit tree

"What have you done?" asked Jérémie accusingly as he gazed at the dozens of branches lying on the snow. I gave him a miffed look that clearly communicated, "I pruned. Duh!" He raised his eyebrows and motioned again at the tree in question. There were only THREE branches still attached to its trunk.

In my defense, pruning was not a skill I had planned to learn this year. I believed it was a pointless activity since wild trees produce fruit without ever being cut. I was also afraid of potentially damaging an otherwise healthy tree.... Hey, if it ain't broke, don't fix it, right? Well, it turns out you can do more harm than good by not pruning your fruit trees. Left on their own to grow as they would in nature, they can become congested and unproductive. You need the sun to shine through the tree to ripen your fruit and the wind to carry away fungal spores.

These are some of the reasons I decided to give pruning a try. Here's what I learned: You should never watch a few pruning videos online and then go outside and start chopping. You should also avoid randomly hacking away at your tree until you feel it looks pretty. That is, of course, what I did. I went from one extreme (not wanting to cut anything) to suddenly taking immense satisfaction in the "snip snip" action of the shears.

Chopping branches, as it turns out, is a therapeutic activity. And so, I kept cutting here and there until my tree only had THREE branches left. I may have gotten carried away, but at least I had done one thing right. The branches were positioned in the classic wine glass shape the pruning experts on the YouTube videos advocated.

Unfortunately, upon further research, this shape is not recommended for apple trees, which make up the bulk of my orchard. Instead, they should be pruned to a central leader system. And that's when I realized I should have consulted an expert. Someone with experience who could help me sift through the conflicting pruning advice. Enter Guy Goguen, co-owner of Le Verger Goguen in Cocagne, New Brunswick. He has been pruning fruit trees on his five-acre family run orchard for 45 years. With his help, I was able to cut through the confusion surrounding this mysterious art.

the basics

1. It is very important to use sharp pruning shears. The cuts should be clean without any tearing. Never simply break off a branch by bending or twisting it.

2. Don't prune in November. This was my first mistake, according to Guy. Fruit trees should be pruned in late winter/first week of spring when the tree sap starts flowing. In our area, this is mid-March. Without all of the trees' leaves, you can more easily see what the heck you're doing. And yes, there is also a scientific reason. First, Guy has found that pruning a tree when it's frozen can cause damage. Second, the wound from pruning will only be exposed for a short time before new growth starts again in the spring. Third, by removing unproductive branches in the late winter, when the tree fully awakens in the spring, it can focus

all its energy on the remaining limbs, resulting in amazing, new growth. Bigger trees equal more fruit equal very happy homesteaders.

3. Prune little and often. It is recommended to prune every year, but never more than a third of the tree's new growth. Basically, don't go crazy and prune all but three branches from your tree.

4. It's best to remove limbs when they are young (small). The smaller the cuts you make, the smaller the wounds the tree has to heal.

5. Dead, damaged, and diseased (the three D's) branches should be removed first. You should also be on the lookout for any branches that are crossing and/or rubbing as this can cause damage to the tree's bark.

6. Remove the shoots called suckers, which often grow from the base of the tree. Your trees are most likely grafted, which means they have been joined with the rootstock of a hardier (but much less desirable) variety. These suckers will take energy away from fruit production from the tree grafted on top. Take these suckers out whenever they appear.

7. You should also remove what's called water sprouts, thin shoots that grow straight up from the branches. These sprouts most likely will never produce much fruit.

8. The same goes for downward growing branches. They will not only develop few fruit buds, but they will shade your productive branches.

9. Prune to completely remove limbs that are growing inward toward the centre of the tree.

10. Be on the lookout for narrow crotches. This occurs when two branches originating from the same trunk or limb grow almost parallel together. These are weak points that could even cause the tree, under a heavy fruit load, to split open and die prematurely. You can either cut the least desirable branch or, if possible, use limb spreaders (I've also seen orchardists use clothespins) to set the branches at a better angle. A rule of thumb is that crotches at a 90- to 60-degree angle are acceptable, but anything less should be pruned.

11. You may also spot what is called a whorl. These are several branches that all grow from the same point. Remove them to prevent overcrowding.

pruning a young fruit tree

When should you begin pruning your tree? The moment after you plant it. I didn't do this, but I wish I had. It's an important first step to establishing your tree's shape.

There are three different structures used for pruning fruit trees — central leader, modified central leader, and the vase or open centred. Most of my trees are apples. After the unfortunate pruning accident I described above, I now know I should use the central leader system, which is Christmas tree or pyramid-shaped.

When you first plant a bare root apple tree, trim the top to about knee-height (32 inches from the ground) at a 45-degree angle away from the bud. Any branches below 24 inches from the ground should also be cut off at the edge of the collar.

Note: Never leave a stub. You don't want to leave more than ⅛ inch of wood outside the branch collar. Why? The wound will take longer to heal, increasing the risk of disease.

Any branches along the trunk above 24 inches should be cut back to two to four inches (there should be no more than two buds on each stub) to help develop strong, thick branches.

how to tell your tree what to do

When I started pruning, I didn't know the difference between a fruit bud and a growth bud. Actually, I didn't know much of anything, but I really wished I had known the difference between these two buds so I had more control over whether my tree produced more fruit or simply new growth. The fat, rounded buds are fruit buds and the growth buds are thinner and lay flat against the stem. If you want to favour new growth, reduce the amount of fruit buds. And if you want to favour more fruit, reduce the amount of growth buds.

TIP New growth will shoot out from the same direction that the bud is pointing, so choose your bud wisely.

As the tree grows, you hope to find four branches spaced evenly around the trunk. (I say hope because as I described above, some of mine now only have three.) These are called your scaffold branches. Over time, you should have several tiers of these scaffold branches, spaced about two feet apart, up the trunk of the tree. So, for example, if tier No. 1 is two feet above the ground, tier No. 2 should be five feet above the ground and so on.

The main trunk of your tree is called the "central leader" and just like any well-organized team, there should only be one. Any competing leaders that arise near the top of the tree should never be allowed to grow taller than the uppermost bud of the leader.

And that's it. Simple, right? OK, I know all this information may sound daunting, but once you actually prune a couple of trees, you'll quickly get the hang of it. You might even find it so much fun that your husband has to shout at you to stop before you cut down all your trees.

project 47

how to grow lemons indoors

I have a secret to share about lemon trees. They don't just produce delicious lemons. They also produce tiny, delicate white blossoms that give off the most delectable, sweet, citrusy-floral perfume. And despite what you may have read online in other articles, in my experience, they are EASY to grow indoors — if you grow the right variety and treat it well and don't mind waiting up to nine months for the fruit to ripen. That's right. NINE looooonnnngggg months! Before I get into the details of how to grow a lemon tree indoors, here are four reasons why you should have one:

four reasons to grow a lemon tree indoors

Your home will be filled with a sweet, citrusy floral fragrance

I had no idea lemon trees gave off such a wonderful, fresh lemon aroma and now I couldn't imagine not having this spectacularly scented treat in my home. And not just once a year. My two lemon trees like to bloom several times a year. It's like having your own all-natural scented plug in. But better. Because you get to eat lemons!

Lemons so fresh and delicious you won't want to buy the ones from the supermarket

Or at least that is what I'm led to believe because I'm still waiting for my ONE, humongous lemon to turn yellow so I can harvest it. I have had this tree for a year and although there are other small ones beginning to grow, this is my first fully grown lemon. It's the size of a grapefruit and weighs roughly two pounds. But it's still green. Apparently, it can take up to nine months for them to ripen, which they do from the inside out. Why is my lemon so big? It's a Ponderosa lemon, which is supposed to have an intense lemon flavour making them excellent for juicing (read: lots of homemade, gourmet lemonade) and cooking, or just squirting into your evening tea.

Each lemon also has an abundance of lemon skin for zest. Fresh lemon blueberry muffins, anyone? Or maybe lemon cheesecake? Or lemon zest pasta? The point is you will have the freshest lemons on hand for whatever recipes you invent. I chose the self-fertile Ponderosa lemon tree because it isn't too fussy about soil type and does well in containers or so the tag told me. Fortunately, the tag did live up to its claims.

I also grow a Meyer lemon bush indoors. No, it's not a tree, but in comparison to my "one lemon wonder tree," after one year this little bush has several lemons growing on it, and it is supposed to produce year round. Meyer lemons are also juicier and less acidic than a typical lemon.

> **NOTE**
> I wish this was an exotic green coloured lemon from a faraway land, but no. It's an unripe one. It takes nine months for the fruit to ripen.

Easy To Grow

I'll be honest. I didn't have high hopes for my lemon tree experiment. I had read it is really hard to grow lemon trees indoors, but for once something I tried was actually easy. Of course, I had to mark down this occasion — The Old Walsh Farm tried something and it worked, and they didn't injure any body parts (or their animals' body parts), get stung, cry, or … you get the picture.

Lemon Trees Are Beautiful

Indoor plants seem to be all the rage in décor these days so if you're going to plant something in your home anyway, why not consider a lemon tree? They are definitely beautiful with their dark, green glossy leaves, lacy pink and white flowers, and bright yellow lemons — well, at least nine months from now when my lemons turn yellow.

how to grow a lemon tree indoors

Plant It
I bought my lemon trees from The Green Barn Nursery and then simply filled a large pot with Pro Mix Organic All Purpose Potting Soil and planted them in it. Simple.

Give It Sunshine
You must place this tree in a south-facing window — or else. No ifs, ands, or buts. You will NOT get any lemons and your tree will not thrive if it does not receive the proper light. Lemons love sunshine — the more, the better.

Feed It
I keep the tree well fed throughout the year with fertilizer. I use worm castings as well as Neptune's Harvest Organic Fish Seaweed Fertilizer. Fish and seaweed are some of the world's best natural fertilizers. You simply mix one ounce of the fertilizer in a gallon of water and pour evenly around your tree.

Water It
I water my lemon tree when I remember. There is probably some secret formula for this, but I check on the tree every now and then and water it if the surface of the soil seems dry. Although I don't do this, you could also put a saucer filled with pebbles and water underneath your plant to raise the humidity for this tropical tree.

So what are you waiting for? Lemon trees are easy to grow, produce delicious fruit, make your home smell like a bouquet of lemon flowers — why the heck not give this a try? In about a year, you can enjoy one big, ginormous green lemon. It will all be worth it.

project 48

sweet lemon honey & thyme cough syrup

Just a spoonful of honey helps the medicine go down, the medicine go down, the medicine go down. ... Except in this case the honey is the medicine and this cough syrup is most likely the best-tasting remedy you've ever had. The kids even tried faking a few coughs just to enjoy a spoonful. OK, maybe my husband and I suddenly came down with severe coughs, too, and were required to slurp down a few tablespoons before bed. So, yes, it tastes delicious, but you're obviously wondering ... does it work? This remedy is so effective that after making this cough syrup in the fall, none of us got a single cough all winter long. So, no, I have no idea if it works, but it should.

Honey is a well-known cough suppressant recommended by doctors. According to a study in the Archives of Pediatrics and Adolescent Medicine where they compared honey, honey-flavoured dextromethorphan (a traditional cough suppressant), and no medicine at all, honey was the winner. It was the most effective remedy in relieving coughing in children with upper respiratory tract infections. (Note: Honey should never be given to children under the age of 1.)

The other key ingredient in this recipe is thyme, which, according to WebMD, may soothe muscle spasms such as coughing. The last ingredient is lemon. I'm not sure if lemon will help relieve your cough, but the fruit is full of immune boosting vitamin C and, in any case, is a tasty addition.

What I love most about this remedy is that I can produce all the ingredients on my farm. Honey from my bees, lemons from my indoor tree, and thyme from my windowsill herb garden. Although this recipe only lasts about a month in the fridge, when a coughing attack strikes, you can easily whip it up in minutes with ingredients you hopefully have stored in your cupboard or growing in your home.

ingredients

- ½ lemon, chopped
- ½ cup honey (raw is best, but regular will do)
- a handful of fresh thyme sprigs
- 1 pint of water (2 cups)

instructions

1. Place the lemon in the pint jar and cover with the honey. The honey will macerate the lemons and draw out liquids which taste so delicious!

2. Meanwhile, toss the thyme leaves into a saucepan and cover them with the water.

3. Bring the water to a gentle simmer and reduce it to half, about a cup of tea.

4. When the tea is reduced and cooled a bit, strain the sprigs and leaves, add the liquid to the pint jar and stir it well.

5. Give it a shake and use a spoonful as needed.

6. Store your homemade cough syrup in the refrigerator for about a month.

NOTE
This simple home remedy is from the excellent homesteading blog, Reformation Acres (www.reformationacres.com).

DECEMBER

I had BIG Hallmark-like expectations for our first Christmas on the homestead. We were going to feast, celebrate, and ring in the New Year with peace, joy, and homemade everything. Because isn't that what homesteaders do? Send out personalized handmade cards, wrap gifts in tree bark and spruce clippings, and prepare a mountain of from-scratch deliciousness?

Maybe they do. But it turns out this family most definitely does not. Instead we decided to take on more farm renovations a few weeks before Christmas. Who starts tearing their home apart shortly before their holiday guests are scheduled to arrive on the farm? Me. That's who.

We were in the midst of "trying to" install a woodstove to provide much-needed heat in our drafty farmhouse. But somehow, I ended up with TWO woodstoves (neither one installed) in my living room because the first one we bought was the wrong size. Also adorning my living room floor was an oversized cast-iron sink from the kitchen. As you can imagine, it all made for a nice Christmasy atmosphere.

And although I had plans to bake dozens of holiday treats, instead I warned guests that I would be serving tea and pickles. Because as you may remember, I fermented cucumbers a few months ago — only I made far too many, leaving almost no room available in my fridge for Christmas goodies. (The pickles turned out great, by the way. Except you might not want to try the cinnamon and cloves combination. Apparently, they're not to everyone's taste.)

So, it may not surprise you that I found myself with only days left before Christmas without a single baked good, gift, or card. I watched my holiday spirit evaporate as I frantically grabbed toys and decorations from store shelves. Never again!

You can't do EVERYTHING — not now and not at any time of the year. You may think you can, and even give it your best effort (points to herself), but there is a very good chance you'll burn out.

You don't want ashes of wasted or failed efforts. You want the warm glow of memories well spent with your family. And there is only one way to achieve this. You have to simplify Christmas to "good enough." No more grand expectations. No more guilt.

We bought a living potted tree for the living room and let the kids decorate it however they wanted. I even resisted the temptation to rearrange the ornaments after they went to bed. We limited the decorations to the living room. We made one baked good — gingerbread cookies.

In the past, we splurged on toys for the kids. Now we've pared down the Santa wish list to: Something they want, something they need, something to wear, something to read, something to make, something to eat. And then we actually relax and slow down. We lock the kids outside and sit by the uninstalled woodstove and enjoy a hot beverage in peace. I'm joking of course. We would never lock the kids outside — at least not for

more than five or 10 minutes before joining them to throw snowballs, make snowmen, and savour these last few days before ringing in another year and inevitable birthdays.

Christmas is busy enough without having the added pressure of learning new skills. I didn't even take on four this month. Instead I learned to make butter and candles, both projects that can be done in less than 30 minutes and which could double as gifts or decorations for your holiday table.

And as we do at the end of every year, we reviewed our finances. Boring, you say? I'm one of those nerdy people who loves to crunch numbers. There is nothing like a goal and a good ol' budget to keep you from buying a herd of dairy cows, a dozen pigs, a flock of turkeys, an elephant, and a couple monkeys. What can I say? I love animals.

Although I stay at home and farm with the kids, Jérémie works full time off the homestead. This isn't ideal, but this is the plan until we can find a way to earn more income from our farm. But I have to say … having all our family home together is a goal worth budgeting for. Don't you agree?

How to Make Butter

Homemade Candles

Homesteading with Little Humans

Get Out of Debt

project 49

how to make butter

Most people would make butter on their kitchen counter. I made this recipe crouched on the living room floor. This is where I had been preparing most of my meals because there weren't any power outlets in our kitchen. This is just one more oversight on our part when we bought our farmhouse and one more item on our ever growing to-do list. Normal people may see this unfortunate predicament as an excuse to order fast food. But not me. Oh no! Instead, I thought this would be the perfect time to learn to make butter.

Now you may be thinking I'm one crazy homesteader, but the truth is, making butter is so easy, all it takes is a few minutes and two ingredients. Your whole kitchen could be falling apart and you could still whip up rich, smooth, luxurious butter. And then it doesn't matter what your kitchen looks like because you'll be too busy making bread and buttery love to even notice.

ingredients

- 2 cups room temperature, heavy or whipping cream
- salt

instructions

1. Pour your cream into a blender leaving enough space at the top so you don't have cream splashing all over your floors ... errr, I mean your counter.

2. Set the speed to medium. If you are using a Vitamix blender, turn the dial to variable 3. Within a few minutes the cream will have thickened to whipped cream. Continue blending. You'll have to stop the machine and scrape down the sides of the container with a spatula every few minutes until you see the mixture starting to "break" and a delicious pool of buttermilk has formed. Pour off the buttermilk into a jar and save it for pancakes.

If you don't have a blender, you can also make butter by hand. I tried this method when the kids were bouncing around the kitchen asking to "help" make supper. Simply put cream in a jar and tell them to shake it until clumps of butter start to form. This activity will keep them busy for at least 10 minutes if you're lucky.

3. Rinse the butter under cool water and then hand-squeeze out any remaining buttermilk. Otherwise, your butter will quickly go rancid. If you don't like using your hands, enclose it in cheesecloth and twist one end until all the buttermilk has drained out.

4. You don't have to salt your butter but it does help preserve it. I dusted mine with some fancy pink Himalayan salt and hand mixed it in. You can then shape your butter however you like. I filled up a mould and popped it in the freezer. Once frozen, it comes out easily. If not, run it under warm water for a few seconds. And voilà! Your Christmas morning holiday table will now be the envy of every homesteader on the block.

project 50

homemade candles

There were only days left before Christmas and I still had gifts to purchase, which meant I still had wrapping to do, which meant ... no, I wasn't ready for the holidays. But I did manage to complete another project amongst the chaos of the season — emergency candles. And no, they're not called emergency candles because we'll have to call 911 when our house burns down, as my husband jokingly (I think?) pointed out. Because I'm thrifty and I don't like anything to go to waste, I made these emergency candles out of lard. It's a heck of a lot cheaper than soy or beeswax. In fact, it's often thrown away so why not put it to good use?

Fun fact: I'm also known to use lard or to even save leftover bacon grease to later use as a moisturizer. So, if you happen to meet me and think you smell bacon, you're not crazy — it's just my cream.

emergency candles

- lard
- wax adhesive or hot glue
- natural wicks and wick stands
- candle holders
- pencils
- essential oils (optional)
- toothpicks

instructions

1. Melt lard in a double-boiler over low heat.

2. Meanwhile apply hot glue or wax to the base of your wick stands and attach them to the bottom of your candle holders. Use two pencils or whatever you have on hand to hold the wicks straight and steady as you pour the lard into your holders.

3. Once the tallow has melted, remove it from the heat and allow the lard to cool slightly (not harden). Stir in essential oils and then pour (reserve some of the liquid for the re-pour in the next step) into your holders.

4. Once the lard has cooled, use a toothpick to poke a couple holes around the wick. Then reheat the remaining lard and re-pour onto the surface. This helps create a smooth candle top and eliminate cracks.

5. Let cool for 24 hours before lighting and trim the wicks to about ¼ inch.

I hope you don't have to burn the midnight lard trying to get everything done before the holidays, but I do hope you enjoy these natural, toxin-free emergency candles.

project 51

homesteading with little humans

How do you homestead with kids? You don't. You drag your crew along for the ride and hope for the best. And then you try really hard not to scream when they run through your vegetable garden and trample your seedlings. You try not to discourage them from helping around the farm even after they've collected and broken so many eggs you've lost count. You try to summon all your patience when baking cookies ends in one kid dumping peanut-butter dough over the other's head. And sometimes you give up and ship them off to Grandma and Grandpa's house so you can get some real work done.

No one will tell you homesteading is easy. But with kids? Well, I imagine it's a lot like trying to swim with two monkeys break dancing on your back. It's slow. There are times when you feel like knocking those crazy animals into the water. And there are moments when you think you're going to drown. But you plunge full steam ahead because 1) You love those little rascals something fierce, and 2) You believe teaching these skills to your children is your life's most important work.

And that's what you have to remind yourself every morning when your son gets up at 5 a.m. and jolts you awake by jumping on your head, when your daughter cuts a hole in her window screen so she can better see the stars, or when they both decide to take a bath in a giant mud puddle and get so filthy you have to dig mud out of their ears.

This is parenting. This is homesteading with kids. And it is the most beautiful, chaotic, crazy, poopy, messy, imperfect life I imagine there is and I wouldn't change a thing. Well, maybe there are a few things I could do without like wiping bums or reminding them it is not OK to pee outside where our neighbours can see them.

Unfortunately, I haven't totally figured out this homesteading and parenting gig. I just do. And somehow, we managed to keep our kids alive and learn 52 homesteading skills in one year. So here are my top tips for keeping your sanity while getting (most of) your homesteading work done.

Let them make a mess

Throughout this book, you'll find pictures of the kids participating in whatever skill I happen to be working on, from making pickles and yogurt, to learning to knit, and starting seeds indoors. Not only is everybody much happier when they are taking part, they enjoy the challenge as much as I do.

Now I'm not saying it is easy to have little helpers and there are times when you may feel tempted to do these projects alone, but don't. Not only won't they learn anything, but this is likely the age they will be most interested in taking part. So invite your 8-year-old to attend a "learn to knit" class with you, encourage your 4-year-old to help you plant peas in the garden, and then ignore the imperfections and embrace the mess. These are memories in the making for you — and for them!

Be flexible

Of course, there are some homesteading tasks your children likely won't be able to participate in. In this case, you're going to have to get creative with your time. I used to cram these activities into naptimes. Now I usually do them in the evenings after they're asleep. In the summer, you'll find me happily working in the garden or planting trees late into the evening. If there's an emergency, like when my bees swarmed, for example, I bring out the TV (for the kids, not the bees). Sometimes you gotta do what you gotta do to get 'er done.

Lower your expectations

This is probably the most important thing you can do as a homesteading mama. I quickly learned to chop my to-do list in half. Why? Because everything takes twice as long when little hands are involved. And, if you're like me, you'll feel discouraged if you don't get the hundred things on your to-do list crossed off. So each night write down one, two, or maybe even three of the most important things you want to accomplish the next day, and focus on those. Anything else you get done is a bonus.

Find their strengths

It's easier to get your kids interested in homesteading when you can involve them in something they love. For Christmas, I gave my 8-year-old daughter, who loves to bake, a cookbook. I made sure I had most of the ingredients on hand and then let her loose in the kitchen. To my amazement, she baked an apple pie — and it was delicious! Since then she has experimented with several other recipes and is a big help come meal time.

My son, on the other hand, loves tools. Give him a hammer, nails, and some wood and he can keep himself busy for 20 minutes. Hey, that's a long time for a 3- or 4-year-old! When I'm working in the garden, I hand him a shovel or trowel, and he's happy to dig for worms (which he feeds to the chickens) alongside me. If we're moving rock, or compost, or soil, he'll help fill the wheelbarrow and cart the goods to their destination — at least for a little while.

Give them chores

You're going to need help around the homestead so if your children are old enough, it's time to employ them. My children help with collecting eggs, feeding the chickens, planting and harvesting crops, watering indoor plants, and, with a little bribing, will even do laundry and pull weeds. I can't say they are always thrilled about doing these chores (or that they do them perfectly), but I think it's important they start learning these life skills now so when the time comes for them to fly the coop, they'll already be old pros — at least that's the pep talk I give them before chore time.

Keep teaching — even when you think they're not listening

Now, there may be moments when you think your kids aren't learning a thing. But hang in there because they may just surprise you. One day we were walking to the park and my daughter spotted an older man pulling dandelions from his front lawn. She stopped and explained to him that our bees needed those flowers for food. It was spring and I had recently explained that dandelions were one of the first food sources for the bees. Hallelujah! My kids are listening, and watching, and learning. So don't give up! Your efforts will pay off.

Are you still confused? Me too. Homesteading with kids is the craziest, and hardest, and yet the most fulfilling and rewarding work I've ever done. You'll laugh, you'll cry, you'll wipe boogers, and you'll feel proud … oh, so proud as you watch your kids learn to knit, learn to preserve foods, learn to garden, and learn where their food really comes from. And that's the reason I dragged them into this adventure and why I'd do it all over again.

project 52

getting out of debt

Have you seen the lists? You know, the ones with hundreds of ideas to make money from your homestead? Sell some eggs, sell some wool, sell some honey. ... By the time you get to the end of these lists it's easy to think you could make millions from your little homestead. After giving some of these ideas a try, I can tell you it's not impossible to earn an income from your farm. BUT ... it takes both money and time before you can enjoy the fruits of your labour. Do you know what's even easier?

Reducing your expenses. Think about it. No one is going to tax you on the money you stop spending. You don't have to declare the money you saved to the IRS. This is free moola for the taking every single month for the rest of your life. You just have to find it, which means, yes, you have to make one of those dreaded budgets and keep track of where all your nickels and dimes are going. It's a time-consuming job to be sure. But it's also exciting! You're about to be crowned the almighty King or Queen of your earnings. You will be able to make your dollars work for you. You just have to be willing to make the right moves.

First, you'll have to come face to face with the truth. Your budget will quickly help you uncover just how much you're really spending on gas, groceries, clothes, gifts, entertainment, electricity, etc. (I use Gail Vaz-Oxlade's free worksheet online, www.gailvazoxlade.com.) Warning! The numbers may shock you. But don't let them stop you in your tracks. There is likely something you can do about nearly everything in your budget — if you really want to. Not everyone is willing to make the necessary sacrifices. This is the moment you discover if you're really cut out for the life of a homesteader, because there are hundreds of ways to save money. You don't have to be a stock market analyst, investment wizard, or financial genius. I know this because I'm not. And our family still managed to pay off all our debts and cut back on our spending. I moaned and I groaned and sometimes even wallowed in self pity when I had to drive around town in a car with multiple dents in the side and a broken door handle. But we did it. Because we're ruthless.

Take food, for example. This expense can add up quickly especially if you enjoy organic, whole, unprocessed, non-GMO, REAL foods. But even if we didn't grow any of our own, we could still eat an organic diet for less than $100 a week. How? We made another budget and priced out meals. Sounds extreme? Yes, it is. But it was a heck of a lot easier (although not as rewarding) than raising our own chicks and eventually selling enough eggs so we could eat our own for free.

Cutting expenses and paying off debt is not as fun as getting a flock of sheep, or a herd of goats, or planting your first garden, but it will help you raise the "extra" money you'll need to be able to invest in these other more exciting homesteading activities.

Yes, homesteading can save you money, but not usually from the beginning. Just like starting a business, you'll have to make investments in fencing, livestock, beehives, seeds, repairs, feed costs … you've been forewarned!

So keep cutting back. Lower your insurance or phone rates by calling around and comparing prices. Lower car expenses by cutting back to one vehicle or — even better for you urban homesteaders — getting rid of the car altogether. Make your own bread, make your own yogurt, and make your own soap. Learn to do repairs yourself.

Soon, this will turn into a game. No, really! You'll find yourself daydreaming of new ways to save money. We retrofitted an old shed that had been rotting into the ground into a coop for our chickens. Instead of buying new windows for our farmhouse, Jérémie refurbished them and installed storm windows. We used free pallets to make our kitchen cupboards. We used free pallets to make a couple raised beds for my garden. When the kids accidentally broke the sink and vanity in our bathroom, we made a new one from a second-hand sink and legs that we cut from an old, broken table we had saved. When you have very little funds, you will get creative, and you may even surprise yourself by what you can achieve.

But what about the Joneses, you say? They're miserable, in debt up to their eyeballs, and they're certainly not homesteaders, so don't even dare compare yourself. Be proud of your beat-up old car (if you happen to own a special vehicle like mine), be proud that you don't have any debt, be proud that you get to live the life you always dreamed about.

One of your big looming expenses is likely a mortgage or rent. We built our former home ourselves so when we sold it, we were able to do so at a profit allowing us to buy our homestead debt free. This is not possible for everyone obviously, but that doesn't mean you have to be stuck with a mortgage. I would urge you to consider renting out a part of your homestead. Rent out a section, rent out a room, rent out part of the barn, rent out some of your land, start a bed and breakfast — whatever you have that you can rent, do it. This is passive income that will allow you to stay on the farm and do what you love while paying your bills.

Renting out half your homestead to another family is a particularly good idea. Not only will you allow another family to enjoy the homesteading lifestyle, but you can form a partnership. There will likely come a day when you want to leave your farm. (I know. It may be hard to believe.) Maybe it's just to go camping with the kids for a weekend or visit relatives in another state. As partners, you can offer to take care of each other's livestock at no cost to either family. This is a much better arrangement than hiring a stranger who isn't familiar with your animals and their unique personalities.

Those with children may also enjoy the benefit of having another family on the farm. Since homesteaders are often located far from neighbours, it's a huge benefit to have other kids close by to play with your own. What I really mean to say is they can keep each other busy while the parents get some work done.

Of course, you can only save so much money. Then you are faced with the problem of how to make ends meet. Although I wish our family could be completely self sufficient, it is next to impossible to provide everything you need for yourself and your family without spending ANY money. It was challenging enough just learning 52 homesteading skills in a year. I can't imagine learning even more and producing every single thing we need on the farm.

So what do we do? Jérémie works full time while I homestead with the kids until we can find more ways to earn an income from our farm. So, yes, we're back to those lists I referred to at the beginning of this story. But before you jump into any of these ideas, I would urge you to crunch the numbers. Take the time and gather all the information. Take beekeeping, for example. I wanted to sell honey, beeswax, and handmade lip balms and soaps. But when I first did the calculations, we were going to break even in our fifth year. Say what? So my dad volunteered to make our beehives reducing the cost to under $100 per hive. And yet, we would still only be breaking even in four years. Better, but not great. So I redid the calculations. This time instead of beginning with one hive, I started with five. Now in your first year, your bees likely won't produce enough honey to share. But in your second year, you should have your first crop and be able to split your hives into two, which not only doubles the amount of hives you have, but also helps prevent swarming. The result is that in your third year, you're not just breaking even, but turning a small profit. Oh, yeah, baby!

Maybe selling eggs or honey won't make sense at first. Maybe you'll have to make your own beehives, or grow some of your own chicken feed, or do something else. Just take the time to do the calculations first and you'll be happy you did.

I know it's really hard to keep your wallet closed when you see an ad for piglets or an end-of-season garden clearance, but remember ... Step one: Reduce expenses and pay off debt. Step two: Take on homesteading activities that make sense after crunching those numbers. (Warning! Everything seems like a good idea before looking at those cold, hard digits.) Step three: Enjoy and celebrate every small step of your journey. This is not a race. There is no finish line or prize. In fact, there's no end in sight! It's simply a way of life for us (more enlightened folk or so I like to think) who want to become more self sufficient, use less energy, eat more nutritious food, raise our kids in nature, (fill in the blank with your reasons for homesteading), and leave the world (or at least our little slice of it) better than we found it.

So what are you waiting for? Don't let money be the reason you never start that homestead. Go rock it, homesteader!

The Journey Continues

There's a knock at the door. I'm unpleasantly surprised to find a police officer standing on my doorstep. Thanks in part to television, I immediately suspect someone I love has been killed in some kind of untimely accident and I mentally brace myself for the oncoming shock and anguish.

Instead I'm told he has a report about six LARGE ducks terrorizing the neighbourhood. I am shocked all right. But for the wrong reasons.

"Excuse me?" I ask as I look at my flock cuddled together for their afternoon nap under our pine tree. I had no idea they had ever wandered from our yard.

"You have to keep your ducks on your property," the officer informed me. "I've had a complaint."

I apologize, of course. And reassure him that I will indeed keep my feathered friends from waddling away and scaring our neighbours.

The next day I keep an eye on those rogue ducks and sure enough they've found a source of water in a ditch along our property line. After splashing and having a quacking good time, those curious creatures decide to check out what's happening on the other side of the ditch. I imagine they're hoping to find a pond. But there's just a house with a boring, old lawn. And a teenager with a duck phobia.

The next day I erect a fence where I suspect the ducks must be crossing. There, I think, I've solved the problem. Alas no. That afternoon the police officer once again arrives on my doorstep.

"Where are your ducks?" he immediately asks.

My heart sinks. They're nowhere in sight.

Apparently, the ducks took great pains to get around the fence and back down to their swimming hole.

The next day I erect another fence. This time in a circle around their house so they can't possibly get up to any more ducky shenanigans. Success!

This is the life of a homesteader. There are days when police may arrive on your doorstep and you'll wonder why you ever decided to start a farm. Days when you'll feel like selling your flock and moving back to the city.

But don't do it!

Yes, it's more challenging than I thought. Yes, it's more expensive than I thought. Yes, it's more time consuming than I thought. But it's also more satisfying, more delicious, and more rewarding than I could have ever imagined.

I am ashamed to say my house is still an unfinished mess and my closets have yet to be organized. And although I learned so many new skills in one year, I have not mastered any.

But as I look out my kitchen window, I can see how far we've come. The garden beds are ready to be planted, the bees survived the winter and are happily buzzing among the Horse Chestnut blossoms, the ducks are still trying to escape and the chickens are dust bathing in my flower pots — again.

I live in a different world than I did just a year ago, and I wouldn't trade it for a hundred city lots.

So what's next for the self-taught homesteader? I actually meant to take a break after finishing this quest. To recharge and re-evaluate and give my husband (who thinks this book should have been titled "52 ways to make your husband miserable all while achieving your dreams") a well-deserved repose from my non-stop "little" requests.

But despite the numerous mistakes, setbacks, and failures, I purchased four sheep, a guardian livestock dog, two more beehives, and took on writing this book. This is the simple life you've been dreaming about, right?

So although this tale is at its end, our story isn't over. I hope you'll continue to follow our homesteading misadventures at theoldwalshfarm.com.

And now it's time for me to say goodbye.

I thought I was juggling this book writing and homesteading lifestyle so well. Until I told my daughter I was almost done, and she replied, "Does that mean you'll be able to get up and do things again?" Ah yes! Yes, it does! And so this book ends just like it began. Only instead of exciting you with visions of chicken poop on your front step, I'm off to shovel old donkey doo into my garden. Yup, it's time to get back to the good life.

To be continued ...

Credits

Photographs by Kimberlee Bastien; *page 11:* Getty Images/monicorem; *23:* Getty Images/PoemsAboutMe; *41:* Getty Images/gece33; *42 & 47:* Getty Images/RugliG; *45:* Getty Images (2)/sanjeri, *top,* N-Sky, *bottom; 55:* Getty Images/aluxum, *bottom; 57:* Shutterstock/Oleksandrum, *top,* Getty Images/fermate, *bottom; 91:* Adobe Stock/alexxich; *99:* Getty Images/KarpenkovDenis; *139:* Getty Images/thermorra; *185:* Getty Images/Alfira Poyarkova. *Front cover photographs:* Kimberlee Bastien. *Back cover photograph:* Ruby Rose Photography

Publisher: Bill Uhler
Editorial Director: Oscar H. Will III
Merchandise and Event Director: Andrew Perkins
Production Director: Bob Cucciniello
Special Content Editor: Christian Williams
Special Content Managing Editor: Jean Teller
Special Content Assistant Editor: Jean Denney
Book design and layout: Alex Tatro

Ogden Publications
Topeka, Kansas